The life of Webern

Musical lives

The books in this series will each consider
an account of the life of a major composer,
considering both the private and public
figure. The main thread will be biographical,
and discussion of the music will be integral
to the narrative. Each book thus presents an
organic view of the composer, the music,
and the circumstances in which the music
was written.

Published titles

The life of Bellini JOHN ROSSELLI
The life of Mahler PETER FRANKLIN
The life of Webern KATHRYN BAILEY
The life of Debussy ROGER NICHOLS
The life of Mozart JOHN ROSSELLI

The life of Webern

KATHRYN BAILEY

CAMBRIDGE
UNIVERSITY PRESS

PUBLISHED BY THE PRESS SYNDICATE OF THE UNIVERSITY OF CAMBRIDGE
The Pitt Building, Trumpington Street, Cambridge CB2 1RP, United Kingdom

CAMBRIDGE UNIVERSITY PRESS
The Edinburgh Building, Cambridge, CB2 2RU, United Kingdom
40 West 20th Street, New York, NY 10011-4211, USA
10 Stamford Road, Oakleigh, Melbourne 3166, Australia

First published 1998

Printed in the United Kingdom at the University Press, Cambridge

Typeset in FF Quadraat 9.75/14 pt, in QuarkXPress™   [SE]

A catalogue record for this book is available from the British Library

Bailey, Kathryn.
Life of Webern / Kathryn Bailey.
     p.   cm. – (Musical lives)
Includes bibliographical references and index.
ISBN 0 521 57336 X (hardback) – ISBN 0 521 57566 4 (paperback)
1. Webern, Anton, 1883–1945.   2. Composers – Austria – Biography.
I. Title.   II. Series.
ML410.W33B32   1998
780′.92–dc21
[B]   97–25751   CIP   MN

ISBN 0 521 57336 X hardback
ISBN 0 521 57566 4 paperback

to the memory of my husband, Derrick: had he lived to read this,
it would have been a better book

CONTENTS

ILLUSTRATIONS

Illustrations 1–14 and 16–17 are from the Sammlung Anton Webern, Paul Sacher Stiftung, Basel and are reproduced by kind permission of the Paul Sacher Stiftung.

In 1901 the seventeen-year-old Webern wrote to his cousin Ernst Diez: 'And what about Art, which means everything to me, for which I would be ready to sacrifice myself! What I imagine . . . is just this: . . . that I will . . . live exclusively for art, and not *from* art simply to earn money.' The thoughts expressed in this youthful rapture describe with almost chilling accuracy the life that was to unfold for Webern over the subsequent forty-four years. Ironically Webern, the composer who was to be seen by many as the originator of the hyperintellectualised integral serialism of the decades immediately following his death and whose own music most people found thoroughly bewildering upon first hearing, was by nature an ardent romantic who held feeling – and comprehensibility – to be important above all else in art. Throughout his life he was completely convinced of the validity and the worth of his own work, in the face of continuing denunciation and criticism. His life was spent in poverty as a result of his lack of concern for practicalities, his belief in the value of the brief moments of music he produced never wavering.

Several things are particularly striking about the young Webern: his inability to make decisions and fulfil commitments, his unquestioning loyalty to his teacher Schoenberg (an attitude sometimes carried to the point of absurdity), his absolute belief in the rightness of the direction he was taking in his musical composition. The first of these resulted in a toing and froing in the years 1908–20 that could hardly have been improved upon by Feydeau, with some twenty-seven changes of residence during these years, not including the six postings during his intermittent periods of military service in 1915 and 1916. His feelings towards Schoenberg exhibited all the fervour of a love affair: consider his wish, expressed in 1917, to buy a farm where his family and Schoenberg's could live so that he (Webern) could till the soil and raise food for Schoenberg while he (Schoenberg) composed and carried on his great work. At the same time Webern's conviction of the value of his own work led him to make a number of choices that would seem to have been – and that indeed at the time did seem, to both his father and Schoenberg, to be – quite imprudent.

Webern's love of the Carinthian mountains and the alpine flowers that grew there was an important part of his makeup. The Voralpen were almost an obsession with him, and his love of the peace and solitude to be found there, as well as his fascination with the flora – paralleling his interest in Goethe's theories of the *Urpflanze* – had a direct bearing on his music. Artistically his sympathies lay with the lyric painters and poets of his day, as well as, later, with the strange mystical poetry of Hildegard Jone, whose texts he set exclusively from the time of their meeting in 1926. His idiosyncratic concept of lyricism is an important aspect of his approach to art and music.

Finally, his romantic naïveté led Webern to express a blind faith in the moral rightness of Germany through two world wars, and this, in the case of the second, in spite of the fact that his beloved teacher and many of his closest friends had been forced to emigrate or go into hiding (often with Webern's help), and his own compositions had been banned. Webern's attitude to Hitler and the Third Reich is complex and, to an outsider, perplexing.

The first Webern biography was written in 1966 by Friedrich Wildgans, clarinettist, composer, Professor of Music at the Vienna Academy, and for a time President of the Austrian chapter of the International Society for Contemporary Music (hereafter ISCM), a man who had known Webern for a number of years. It was translated immediately into English.[1] This was followed in 1975 by Hanspeter Krellmann's biography,[2] which unfortunately has never been translated. Both of these works were modest in scale (their respective 185 and 156 pages give a misleading idea of their length, since the Wildgans is set in an expansive typeface, with nearly half of the book devoted to a 'Critical Catalogue of Works', short essays by other people and a bibliography/discography, while a large proportion of the Krellmann is, as indicated in the title, devoted to photographs). Both were based on Webern's diaries and correspondence and various other original documents which were in the archives of the Vienna Stadtbibliothek and Universal Edition, or in the possession of Webern's family and friends, and both are faithful to the materials consulted. Wildgans' picture of Webern is coloured by personal loyalty and by Wildgans' expressed mission of countering what he rightly saw to be widespread misconceptions about the composer and his music. Krellmann's is an objective and excellent compilation of the material available.[3]

Meanwhile, in 1958 (or 1959; his own accounts differ) the German-American pianist and educator Hans Moldenhauer had begun his single-minded and tireless quest for Webern memorabilia. He at first took possession of Webern's death (in the form of an unsolicited personal investigation of the events surrounding that event which resulted in a book, *The Death of Anton Webern*[4]), then in 1961 and the years following proceeded to amass the materials of the composer's life. In this he was greatly aided by Webern's eldest daughter, Amalie Waller, who unilaterally gave him nearly everything of her father's that

[1] *Anton Webern*, trans. Edith Temple Roberts and Humphrey Searle (London: Calder and Boyars, 1966). It was published in German only in 1967 (Tübingen).

[2] *Anton Webern in Selbstzeugnissen und Bilddokumenten* (Reinbek bei Hamburg: Rowohlt Taschenbuch Verlag, 1975).

[3] It is also the most accurate of any to date, according to Maria Halbich-Webern, Webern's second daughter.

[4] *The Death of Anton Webern: A Drama in Documents* (New York: Philosophical Library, 1961).

remained in the family's possession. By 1966 Moldenhauer's personal collection of Webern memorabilia was quite considerable (a catalogue of its contents was published in that year[5]).

In 1978 Moldenhauer, with the assistance of his wife Rosaleen, wrote the definitive biography of Anton Webern, based primarily on the original materials in their possession.[6] This was not a modest effort: its 803 pages touch on just about all there is to know about Webern. It is an unwieldy book: the way in which it is organised and its stultifying comprehensiveness – it is a compendium of dates and documents – make it more useful as a reference tool than as a biography. It is an exasperating experience for someone attempting to get a clear view of chronology, and I have met very few people who admit to having read it 'straight through'. I find Moldenhauer's attitude towards the woman who gave him the family jewels irritating (and so, indeed, does at least one of her sisters): he misses no opportunity, and invents several, of extolling the qualities of Amalie Webern and of identifying her repeatedly as Webern's favourite among his children, while largely ignoring the other three. Moldenhauer's high-profile pursuit of Webernalia and his subsequent sequestering of the results for his own use were off-putting to many, as perhaps was the morbid fascination of his first Webern publication. A readable book that sets out the more important events of Webern's life and dispenses with the mass of details is needed. Something of this sort was offered in 1995 by Malcolm Hayes, but as his only source was Moldenhauer he repeated Moldenhauer's mistakes without giving any new insights on either the man or his music.[7]

---

[5] In *Anton von Webern Perspectives*, compiled by Hans Moldenhauer and edited by Demar Irvine (Seattle: University of Washington Press, 1966).

[6] *Anton von Webern: A Chronicle of his Life and Works* (London: Victor Gollancz, 1978).

[7] *Anton von Webern* (London: Phaidon Press, 1995). I find it curious – and the several people who have contributed to the wider knowledge of Webern biographical information in the last fifty years must find it inexplicable, not to say irritating and irresponsible – that Hayes seems to have looked no further than Moldenhauer, even to the extent of knowing that there is any more to look

In the present book I hope that I have done something more than this. In approaching the project I was determined to read and translate the original materials myself. Since most of the Moldenhauer Webern Archive is now located in the Sacher Stiftung in Basel and the Library of Congress in Washington, and the bulk of the correspondence that was never owned by Moldenhauer is located in New York, Washington and Vienna it is possible to do this. I have seen and transcribed a considerable portion of this material. I have used my own translations of the material that I have seen, and I have endeavoured to use as far as possible photographs and facsimiles that have not been published before, though this has been difficult, particularly in view of the abundance of photographs in the Krellmann book and the publication *Webern 1883–1983*.[8] I have also tried, to the extent that it has seemed germane rather than simply dogmatic, to incorporate portions of the diaries and letters that were not quoted by the Moldenhauers. But one of the results of a considerable time spent in close scrutiny of the Webern materials has been an increased respect for the Moldenhauers and for the really quite monumental work that they did between 1959 and 1978. Early Webern is difficult reading (though a slightly older Webern was the composer of some of history's tidiest music, the young Webern was not a careful writer, and he never quite mastered spelling) and the Moldenhauers give a careful and for the most part accurate reading of *all* of these materials (including a large number of letters that were never a part of their collection and therefore must have been consulted elsewhere) as well as a good eye for the bits that were most important. Their translations are also good, in my opinion: though they often improved the elegance of the original, the meaning has been retained with considerable faithfulness. This

---

at. His Preface begins: 'Anyone writing a biography of Webern at the present time is in the unusual situation of having only one major published source of documentation on which to draw.'

8   A Festschrift for the hundredth anniversary of Webern's birth, edited by Ernst Hilmar with an introduction by Henri Pousseur (Vienna: Universal Edition, 1983).

turned out to be particularly fortunate for me, as I have had to rely on their translations of more of the letters than I had hoped would be the case. Whenever I have used their translation this is indicated in the text. In the end I feel compelled to express my deep respect for their work and its importance for all subsequent Webern studies. Their book is still the comprehensive source on Webern's life and is recommended to anyone who wishes to find out more facts and details.

There remains, however, the need for an accurate and carefully composed small biography in which the approach is scholarly but the apparatus is not, which sets out the chronology of Webern's life clearly, and in which perhaps a few new perceptions about both his personality and his music will be offered and seen to have some value. It is my hope that the present volume will fulfil this need.

I include a short bibliography of works consulted, which will be of interest to anyone wishing to fill in the gaps necessarily left in a volume of the dimensions of this one. In the attempt to keep footnotes to a minimum I refer to a few frequently quoted sources by abbreviations in brackets within the text. The following abbreviations are used in this way:

Berg   Berg, *Letters to his Wife*
BSC   Brand *et al.*, eds, *The Berg–Schoenberg Correspondence*
DAW   Hans Moldenhauer, *The Death of Anton Webern*
HM   Hans and Rosaleen Moldenhauer, *Anton von Webern*
Jone   Webern, *Letters to Hildegard Jone and Josef Humplik*
PNM   Webern, *The Path to the New Music*
Smith   Joan Allen Smith, *Schoenberg and his Circle*
Zem   Zemlinsky, *Zemlinskys Briefwechsel mit Schönberg, Webern, Berg und Schreker*

Complete publishing information for these books can be found in the bibliography. The translations from the Zemlinsky correspondence are my own.

ACKNOWLEDGEMENTS

One of my greatest pleasures during the preparation of this book was meeting Maria Halbich-Webern, Webern's second daughter. Frau Halbich, who bears a great physical resemblance to her father (and who says that everyone, especially her mother, always remarked that she was like him in other ways as well), is a very spirited and engaging person, and spending time with her felt uncannily like meeting her father first-hand, though she is now more than twenty years older than he ever got to be. If my thoughts about Webern have shifted slightly simply as the result of observing her (and they have) I make no apology: I believe that such intuitions are not to be repudiated. I wish to thank her for her generosity, first of all in spending considerable time in conversation with me and secondly in allowing me to transcribe her father's correspondence and to reproduce both the Jone painting used on the book cover and photographs that once belonged to her family. For permission to use the photographs, which are now part of the Webern Nachlass of the Paul Sacher Stiftung in Basel, as well as material from the eight notebooks and five sketchbooks also in that collection, Webern's letters to Ernst Diez, the Dallapiccola recollections and various other letters and documents, I am also extremely indebted to that institution, and particularly to Felix Meyer, who has been, as always, helpful and accommodating. I wish to express my thanks to Lawrence Schoenberg and the Schoenberg family for their kind permission to see and use letters from the

Webern–Schoenberg correspondence, and to the Stadt- und Landes-bibliothek in Vienna, where I was shown many of these letters, as well as a ninth notebook, the existence of which I had not been aware of previously.

Many people have helped me in various ways: Inge Dupont, Vanessa Pintado and Katherine Reagan at the Pierpont Morgan Library in New York and Christine Dreier, Sabine Hänggi-Stampfli, Ingrid Westen, Tina Kilvio Tüscher and Johanna Blask at the Sacher Stiftung in Basel were all extremely generous with their time and showed remarkable patience. The weeks spent in these two libraries will always be remembered as most pleasant times. Theophil Antonicek, archivist at the University of Vienna, sent me unpublished information about Webern's university career and Rosemary Moravec-Hilmar, curator of music sources and documents at the Austrian National Library, offered me a copy of her own extensive list of the Berg–Webern correspondence, and pointed me in several of the right directions. David Lewin of Harvard University was very generous with his reminiscences about Steuermann, and William Drabkin of the University of Southampton helped with some difficult translation. My visits to Basel and Vienna were made memorable by the great kindness of Ingrid and Martin Metzger and Helga Vedral, to all of whom I am very grateful.

The last months of work on this book were done at what turned out to be an extremely difficult time for me, and in the event I was unable to do personally some of the things that I had intended to do. I am most grateful to all those people who helped me to fill in the gaps. Both Christopher Hailey and Wayne Shirley were very generous with information about and reproductions of Webern materials at the Library of Congress in Washington, which I was in the end unable to visit. And I owe a particular debt of gratitude to Morten Solvik, who became my man in Vienna, sorting out a miscellany of loose ends and tracking down many elusive but necessary things for me with great good humour and efficiency. I am ever grateful to Allen Forte for his constant encouragement, and for letting me use the picture of Mittersill.

I wish especially to thank my son, Gauvin Bailey, and my daughter, Sara Watts, for their careful reading and their thoughtful discussion of the typescript and its contents, as well as for their suggestions, all of which have been taken to heart and carefully considered and most of which have been incorporated. Their help was invaluable. And, finally, I am very grateful to Penny Souster for her encouragement and understanding throughout a difficult time.

KATHRYN BAILEY
CAMBRIDGE, 1997

Prologue

At the beginning of December 1945 I happened to visit the house owner Frau Fasching, in whose house Webern had lived. When she knew that I had been a friend of the deceased, she asked me whether I should like to see the house, and she took me to Auholz [Im Auholz 8, in Maria Enzersdorf, the Weberns' last Vienna address]. Of the beds only the iron frames remained; many of the floor boards had been burned as fuel, as well as odd pieces of the furniture. Parts of the library were on the cellar stairway, where they had been piled, in spaces between old broken fruit jars. A score of Schoenberg's *Gurrelieder* (a conducting score), books, pictures were piled in a veranda of which the windows had been smashed. Many of the book covers were in tatters, or were sodden or crumpled. She [Frau Fasching] took me to the little garden house, through the roof of which the rain had drenched letters that were strewn about there. On a strip of the lawn the remnants of ashes could be seen: there scattered letters had been burnt. The rest the house owner had stuffed into coal sacks to use as kindling for her stove. I asked her to let me go through the coal sacks. There I found, mixed up with dirt, bones, dead mice, epaulettes and uniforms, upwards of a thousand letters from Webern to his wife, manuscripts, sketches, several hundred letters from Alban Berg, Arnold Schoenberg, Alma Mahler, Marx and so on. I offered to return all the things that I have described here to Webern's widow if she would visit Mödling. The letters from Berg and Schoenberg she asked me to put in order for their eventual publication. This task will be finished soon. The

1   The garden house in Maria Enzersdorf in 1944.

Weberns' daughter-in-law had removed the library and the further
remains of books by car in the previous year. Presumably everything
that was saved at that time, including Webern's grand piano, is now
either with the daughter-in-law or at the home of Webern's widow in
Mittersill bei Zell am See, Burkhalter 31. The letters in the probably
twenty coal sacks were naturally completely crumpled, much of the
ink had run, many had been gnawed at by mice, and everything was
all mixed up, with the several pages of individual letters in this or that
sack. In many cases only fragments had survived. Another portion
of the letters had been thrown on the coal heap, along with letters
belonging to the other occupants of the house. The work of sorting
that was done in the cellar where there was only a candle for light
took many days, that of the coal sacks something like two weeks. It
was unspeakably sad to see this devastation of such precious things.

Thus were the home and belongings of Anton Webern – composer,
conductor and teacher; mountain climber, nature-lover and human
being – described by Dr Werner Riemerschmid – actor, poet and
brother-in-law of Webern's close friend Josef Hueber – in March 1947,
some eighteen months after Webern's death.[1] There are a great many

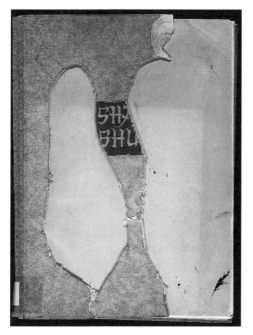

2 Cover of an art book from Webern's personal library from which shoe soles
   were cut by soldiers billeted in the Weberns' house in Maria Enzersdorf in
   1945.

things about the end of this life that can only be described as 'unspeakably sad'.

Webern took a rather long time to 'grow up': though he wrote
music from an early age, he was nearly forty when he finally settled
into the conducting career that was to bring him modest recognition
as well as badly needed income. By this time he had already been
struggling for a number of years, with varying degrees of success, to
support a wife and four children. But history was not to be his friend.
Once achieved, this new life would last for only some dozen years
before being severely curtailed by the National Socialists. In 1935,
when he was fifty-two, Webern conducted his last radio broadcast in
Vienna; in the following year he conducted for the last time anywhere.
After the Anschluß in 1938[2] he and his music were on the proscribed

list: Webern, who had all his life been an ardent German nationalist and for whom the sun rose and set in Vienna, could now no longer conduct, nor could his music be either performed or published in Germany or Austria. His professional life was in tatters some years before his personal worldly goods suffered that fate literally.

The death of this peace-loving and scrupulously honest man four months after the war had ended, from the bullet of a soldier who would not have been there had it not been for the black-market activities of Webern's son-in-law, was for him, finally, the last of a series of ironies. For his widow the grief would continue. And for the world, confusion. Confusion about what had really happened in Mittersill, about the fate of his belongings, about what to make of the man and his music.

1   1883–1902 Childhood and school years

I so often make such plans, such beautiful ones – but perhaps I also
suffer delusions of grandeur!

Webern to Ernst Diez, 22 July 1901

Anton Friedrich Wilhelm von Webern was born on 3 December 1883
at the home of his parents, Carl and Amalie (née Geer[1]) von Webern, at
Löwengasse 53a in Vienna's Third District. Though he was the fourth
of five children, two of these – a daughter and a son – had not survived
infancy, the second having died some twenty months before Anton's
birth.

The Weberns were a middle-class family, descended from an
Austrian aristocratic family that had lived in Carinthia since at least
the sixteenth century. The full name, bestowed in the sixteenth century, was Weber Freiherr von Webern; Webern's father dropped the
title 'Freiherr' but retained the 'von', which in turn had to be dropped
in 1918 to conform with an edict forbidding the use of noble titles following the First World War. Though the name 'von Webern' does not
occur for some time after 1918, it reappears on the letterhead of
Webern's personal correspondence dating from the 1930s and 40s, as
well as on some concert programmes from these years. Schoenberg
also used it on letters to Webern written during this time.

Carl von Webern was a mining engineer who was highly regarded
and the receiver of several decorations. He was one of the founders of

3   Carl and Amalie von Webern with their three children, Rosa, Maria and Anton, in the 1890s.

the Mining College in Leoben, from which he later received an honorary doctorate. He held a series of government positions, involving a number of changes of residence. Amalie Geer was the third daughter of a master butcher in Mürzzuschlag, in Styria. The von Webern family lived in Vienna until 1889; Webern's schooling began there. In 1890, when he was seven, his father was promoted to a position that necessitated the family's move to Graz, and four years later a further advance brought them to Klagenfurt. A subsequent promotion, recorded in Webern's diary in May 1902, brought the family back to Vienna, coinciding neatly with Webern's entry into university there.

Carl von Webern had inherited his family's country estate in Lower Carinthia, and, though the family never used it as a permanent residence, the Preglhof was a much beloved retreat and an important focal point of family life for many years. It was surely there that the seeds of Webern's lifelong love of nature were sown and nurtured, and it was there during family gatherings that he spent long hours in the company of his greatest childhood friend, his cousin Ernst Diez, talking about art and poetry and music, and the meaning of life.

Webern's two surviving siblings were sisters: Maria, three years older than he, and Rosa, two years younger. His sister Rosa's memories, written down many years later, after Webern's death, describe a comfortable, happy and unexceptional childhood. The family was close, and she relates a number of childhood incidents in which her brother emerges as a child who loved nature, possessed a vivid imagination and was sensitive to the point of being nervous – all prominent attributes of the mature Webern. She also writes, predictably, of his early musical interests. The child she describes was not a Mozart, but a typical toddler sitting beside his mother as she played the piano and attempting to imitate her, later asking for his favourite tunes (from *Hansel and Gretl* and, unexpectedly, *Lohengrin*) and singing along ('with complete accuracy', according to his sister), dancing happily with his young sisters to music from the puppet theatre, and receiving at successive Christmases a toy drum, a trumpet and finally a violin.

Webern's mother started teaching him to play the piano at the age of five. When the family moved to Klagenfurt in his twelfth year he began lessons with Edwin Komauer, on both piano and cello. His prowess on the latter instrument led to a family trio, with his older sister Maria playing the piano and Rosa the violin ('halfway decently', according to her modest report). It is noteworthy that the composers she names as forming their repertoire are Mozart, Schubert and Beethoven: these composers would continue to occupy positions of dominance throughout the whole of Webern's life. The young Anton's first surviving compositions date from 1899, when he was fifteen. These are, not surprisingly, two pieces for cello and piano.

It was apparently at the beginning of 1900 that Webern began to keep personal notebooks, a custom in which he would continue for most of his life. Nine of these notebooks survive; internal evidence suggests that there were more. The earliest two of these, one of 119 pages and one of 93, were in use simultaneously. The one that bears the number 1 (although the numbers on these books appear to be in Webern's hand they do not accurately represent their chronology: this book was not the first to be used) covers the time from October 1900 to the end of 1906.[2] Poems and miscellaneous bits of prose have been copied into this book, and in it the young Webern wrote out the programmes of concerts that he heard or participated in, along with brief commentaries on the works and the performances. This book also served as a personal diary, containing longer records of performances that were especially important to him during these years; the most notable of these – and one often quoted – is the account of what he optimistically entitled his 'first trip to Bayreuth'. (It was to be, in fact, his only trip to Bayreuth.) The first page of the book is dated 'October 1900, Klagenfurt'. The second notebook is devoted more consistently to the poems and essays of other people, though there are some personal notes – memos rather than reminiscences – here as well. The first date to appear in this book is on page 38; this is the date of a long essay on Richard Strauss' *Don Juan* (pp. 38–51), copied from the *Grazer Tagespost* of 26 January 1900. Since the only things to appear before this are all, like it, the writings of other people, it is reasonable to suppose that this book was begun at the new year and used immediately to record a number of things that Webern had recently found interesting. This book contains very few dates, but the last two entries are a list of all the operas scheduled for performance in Vienna during the 1902–3 season and Webern's schedule of university lectures for that same winter, so it is safe to assume that it was not in use after the spring of 1903, and perhaps not as late as that.

Throughout these early books there is a clear distinction between the handwriting used for the diary entries and that used for the copied material. When he is recording his own ideas, or making notes on events that engage him personally, the young Webern's handwriting is often inconsistent and hurried, a Gothic script that is sometimes quite difficult to read, written variously in ink or pencil. Spelling is somewhat haphazard. But roman script is adopted for copying favourite poems and essays, this is always done in ink, and on these occasions the letters are carefully formed and even. It is the difference between the teenager making hasty notes to record his rapidly changing thoughts and the young student writing meticulously in his copy book.

Musical experiences and thoughts about music dominate these notebooks. The first entry to have been made is a pair of long essays on *Das Rheingold* and *Siegfried* that were copied on pages 1–9 and 10–22, respectively, of Nb2. The same book contains an essay (on pp. 31–3) by Felix Weingartner on Brahms' Second Symphony and the already mentioned piece on *Don Juan*. Interesting as it is to see what the young Webern considered important enough to copy into his journal, it is probably more so to read the records of his own musical experiences. At the age of seventeen, when his home was in Klagenfurt, where concert life was surely less active than it was in the capital, he was already a frequent concert-goer, and in his notebooks he recorded his opinions – with neither hesitation nor apology – of both the works and the performers that he heard. Notebook 1 contains programmes of and commentary on nine concerts that he attended between 29 October 1900 and 10 March 1901 (pp. 6–14), and this is followed by the account of an event that was clearly of considerable significance: a journey to Graz in Easter week of 1901 for a performance of *Tristan and Isolde* (pp. 15–16). No other concerts are recorded until a similar journey to Vienna one year later, this time to see *Götterdämmerung* (the account of this performance is on pp. 24–7 of the same book). The seven pages between these two Easter treats are devoted to poems by Hermann Ubell and Robert Graf, and to an enthusiastic account of Webern's first acquaintance with a Mahler score (all of which we shall return to presently). Nor is any mention of concerts during this missing year (the 1901–2 season) to be found in Nb2. Thus it seems likely that at least one additional notebook must have been in use during the time between 1900 (when surviving records begin) and the autumn of 1902 (when Webern entered university and moved to Vienna, and began once again to record concerts in Nb1), but no others survive from these years.

The result of this apparent loss, of course, is that although we have a good idea of what events shaped Webern's musical life and what his opinions were in the winter of 1900–1, we have no similar record for the following year. During the season that surrounded his seventeenth birthday he made brief but focused records of two chamber music evenings: the first contained an adequate performance of Beethoven's first quartet which however 'left a good deal to be desired' – the Adagio was picked out especially as having given extraordinary pleasure – and an 'absolutely splendid' performance of Brahms' Piano Quartet in G minor, a work described as a 'supremely powerful tone poem', of which 'the first and third movements especially are of great beauty'. The second chamber music evening did not fare so well: it contained a Dvořák quartet (described as an excellent work, but badly played), the Beethoven Septet (which was 'completely messed up in many places') and songs sung by a singer who was described as having 'a few good notes in the middle range' but being otherwise 'quite bad'. This was dismissed as an unsuccessful evening altogether.

On 11 December two instrumental soloists, the violinist Franz Ondříček and the pianist Wilfred Klasen, shared a programme. Webern was entranced. 'He [Ondříček] played simply divinely. An amazing technique, together with the greatest precision, a profound performance. Of the works I liked best Bach's "Air". The pianist is also distinguished. I was delighted with Liszt's B minor Ballade, which Klasen played very beautifully.'

There was a preponderance of singing in the programmes of the season, particularly as most concerts of any type seem to have included some lieder to fill in the gaps, as in the chamber music concert referred to above. Webern reported on four evenings devoted entirely to lieder, all of which he thought successful. Edyth Walker from the Vienna Opera sang 'in a soft, very wide-ranging contralto voice', accompanied 'in an artistic manner' by Webern's teacher, Edwin Komauer. Lilian Sanderson, who possessed 'a facile contralto voice that is evenly balanced throughout her range and a wholly idiosyncratic and wonderful art of declamation', sang 'everything with a warm artistic feeling', and with a disarming modesty that Webern found very winning: 'Her music touches the heart. . . . Each song was a delight'. He was however less than enthusiastic about Sanderson's accompanist, 'a mediocre pianist, who played Chopin, Liszt and Bach with the greatest lack of expression'. The following month Lula Gmeiner, 'sang magnificently, possessing a darker and more beautiful voice than Sanderson', though in the young Webern's opinion she probably did not stand up to Sanderson's standard of presentation. Her pianist received no mention. The only male lieder singer that year was the great Johannes Messchaert, who shared a concert with the pianist Julius Röntgen. Webern described both as powerful artists: Messchaert sang marvellously and stirred the audience; Röntgen, who played Schumann's *Papillons* and a piece of his own, was described as an outstanding pianist, whose accompanying was perfect. The programmes were dominated by Brahms, Schubert, Schumann and Wolf. Lula Gmeiner included songs by Richard Strauss; the only non-German names to be mentioned are Massenet and Rubenstein, the latter appearing on two occasions. A few lesser-known contemporary composers – Löwe, Lange-Müller, Hermann, Sommer – made appearances as well. Songs singled out by Webern as his particular favourites were Wolf's 'Weyla's Song', 'Verborgenheit' and 'Zur Ruh''; Schubert's 'Lindenbaum' and 'Allmacht'; Brahms' 'Waldeinsamkeit' and 'Auf dem Kirchhofe'; Strauss' 'Du meines Herzens Krönelein'.

And, finally, Webern heard three orchestral concerts at the Musikverein, none of them an unqualified success. The playing is only once mentioned in his reports of two concerts in December and March: these two concerts are treated with a brevity worthy of a much older Webern. In December he heard Mendelssohn's 'Lobgesang', described as 'a wholly insignificant though pleasing work', and in March Siegfried's Funeral March from *Götterdämmerung* ('a work of inexpressible beauty') was given what the young Webern described as a perfect performance, followed by H. Hofmann's 'very feeble and ineffectual' *Nornengesang* and a symphony, 'Im Walde' by Raff,[3] which was very much to his liking. The programme of the first of the Musikverein concerts, that of 11 November 1900, in which Webern participated as a cellist, was an unfortunate, though in that day probably not uncharacteristic, combination of the Mendelssohn Violin Concerto, Elsa's Dream from *Lohengrin*, a group of lieder and the first three movements of Beethoven's Ninth Symphony. In his diary Webern was delighted by the Mendelssohn, which he said was played with distinction. But he didn't like the singer, one M. Rainer, who 'sang the soulful, dreamy Elsa's narrative completely without expression' and performed the lieder, which were in any case 'entirely out of place in the programme', crudely. On the whole the Beethoven went quite well: 'the impression I had, as a player, was indescribable. The public, most of whom have no understanding, gave it a completely indifferent reception.'

In this notebook entry one gets only the slightest hint, in the last sentence, of the violent feelings that this concert seems actually to have evoked in Webern. These we read in a longer account which he wrote to his cousin Ernst Diez four days later.

> Last Sunday we had a Musikverein concert, with a programme that was very tastelessly put together, though one might argue whether its greatest fault was one of organisation or one of omission. [The programme] was as follows: 'Elsa's Dream' from *Lohengrin*, Mendelssohn's Violin Concerto and – now comes the absurdity – a few lieder and then Beethoven's Ninth Symphony, without the final movement because of the lack of chorus and soloists. The individual works are, as you know, magnificent, but the juxtaposition is appalling. How can one sing lieder with piano accompaniment in such a large hall, and just before the Ninth Symphony!

No doubt an important element contributing to his disapproval on this occasion was that two of the composers who suffered from this débâcle – Wagner and Beethoven – were composers whom he idolised. To his cousin he goes on to describe the wonders of the Beethoven and to vent his rage at what he sees as the apathy of the audience. This last was to be a lifelong leitmotif.

> The Ninth was played well, in spite of a few scarcely noticeable rough spots which had not been smoothed out because of poorly attended rehearsals. I of course played in the orchestra. But the indifference of the people is stupendous. They must have absolutely no notion of what it means to perform Beethoven's Ninth. In the newspapers there was, neither before nor after, any notice or acknowledgement of the work. The people simply go there, listen as if a salon polka were being played, and go away again without any excitement. If everyone had felt what I as merely one of the players felt! Often I thought – without an exaggeration – that I was about to weep. The first movement is really terrifying, these tones of infinite grief, with such a colossal climax! Then again the moving Adagio. And the Scherzo, so thrilling and again wildly raging, how insanely the kettledrums beat there; it is an infernal dance by which one is completely terrified.[4]

Webern's reverence for Beethoven, already firmly in place at seventeen, would remain a central pillar of his musical life. When he was persuaded to give several series of lectures on musical form thirty years later these would be based largely on structure as handled in the works of Beethoven. His early enthusiasm for Wagner was to wane, but it was of the utmost importance to his musical sensibility throughout his youthful years. The events recorded at greatest length in the early notebooks were performances of Wagner operas: the trips at Eastertime of both 1901 and 1902 and the long-yearned-for trip to Bayreuth given him by his father upon his successful completion of the Gymnasium in 1902. His delight at this gift can be imagined when one observes that he wrote out carefully the complete schedule of Bayreuth offerings for both the 1901 and the 1902 seasons in Nb2.

The importance of the music of Richard Wagner to the young Webern can hardly be overstated. If this early admiration for Wagner seems surprising in view of the exaggerated succinctness that

Webern's own music was to demonstrate only a decade later, it is completely consistent with his aesthetic and emotional makeup, of which an inclination towards heightened feelings and a strong German nationalism were two essential elements.

A third figure who was to be a profound influence on Webern's musical life entered the picture in January of 1902, and again the major portion of Webern's record turns into a diatribe, in this instance against critics. A long entry in Nb1 bearing only the date January 1902 runs as follows:

> I have finally for the first time had a chance to get to know a work of Gustav Mahler, though only on the piano: his Second Symphony in C minor. At first when playing it through I was baffled by the work; then gradually I became more objective and saw that in fact there was much beauty there, particularly in the first movement, which is in general, however, very contrived and bizarre. Nevertheless it seems to me that those spiteful criticisms, such as were raised against his skill on the occasion of the first performance of Mahler's Fourth Symphony, are very unprofessional, that the critic very simply does not or will not understand the composer; the assumption that Mahler writes parody, and makes a joke with his symphonies, or other such notions seem completely absurd to me. In my eyes he appears as a great, inspired conductor and a serious, deeply introspective composer to whom I look up with admiration, and I burn with desire to learn more of his works.

This entry ends with the information that Strauss' *Feuersnot* was performed at the Vienna Opera at the end of the month under Mahler's direction, to highly negative criticism.

To his cousin Ernst, Webern wrote very similar impressions of the Mahler symphony. In a letter written on 20 February 1902 (the date on this letter is written incorrectly as 1901) he says:

> I have finally had the opportunity to get to know one of Mahler's symphonies, in a piano reduction, of course. I liked it very much. The first movement impressed me particularly. Of course if one plays Richard Strauss right after, or vice versa, one notices a big difference.

Strauss' themes are much more splendid, more ingenious, more powerful. Mahler's music makes really an almost childlike impression, despite the quite enormous orchestral apparatus. He uses, for example, two orchestras, no fewer than *ten* horns, five to six of each of the woodwinds. I am terribly curious about his Fourth Symphony.

This letter contains the only extant evidence of a concert in Klagenfurt from the 1901–2 season. Here Webern writes that on the following Monday a Madame Fregi was going to sing 'a magnificent programme' containing, 'among other things, *five* Wolf songs', and that he hoped to be asked to turn pages for her accompanist (again his teacher Komauer) so that he could meet the artist. There is no record of this concert written after the fact.

The young Webern's first recorded Wagner experience was the performance of *Tristan* in Graz in the week before Easter of 1901. Even on this very special occasion his report is surprisingly brief, though such details as the exact time of the train from Klagenfurt to Graz (2.18 p.m.) and the complete cast list are noted. This almost obsessive attention to detail, and in particular to the precise times of arrivals and departures, is a lifelong idiosyncrasy.

The impression was overwhelming. If I were to say what made the greatest effect on me, it was the scene in which the lovers drink the potion, the lovers' duet, Tristan's asking Isolde whether she will follow him into the 'dark-nighted land' and Isolde's answer, and finally the entire third act with its dreadful climaxes. Winkelmann's Tristan is absolutely second to none; his interpretation, especially during the last act, is magnificent. All the rest of the cast, with the exception of Ritter (Marke), were excellent. The orchestra played very beautifully, though I thought the Vorspiel much the best. Sitting in the first row of the parquet and having thoroughly studied the score beforehand, I could savour everything wonderfully, and thus I had an indescribable experience which I shall never forget.

Like many, this account displays a touching combination of youthful exuberance (the description of approximately the second half of the opera as his favourite bit) with a confidence that surely goes beyond his experience (one wonders how the seventeen-year-old seeing *Tristan* for the first time could pronounce Winkelmann's Tristan as second to none!).

One year later a similar trip took Webern to the Hofoper in Vienna for a performance of *Götterdämmerung*. The report is longer this time, taking four pages. Again his description of those scenes that most impressed him gets out of hand: his favourite bits know no end.

> The impression was indescribable; but it could have been even greater had my attention not been distracted by so many other things. In the first place the orchestra, the size of which amazed me. Then the conductor, and the people, the opera and so on. Naturally the performance was inspired. The orchestra played quite beautifully altogether. I admired especially their discipline; the crescendos and decrescendos were simply miraculous. From the beginning I liked Schmedes best. The scenery was very beautiful. The closing scene: the conflagration in the hall of the gods,—sadly I could not see, since I sat in the second row of a box. Of the whole 'Ring' *Götterdämmerung* is my favourite. Particularly the orchestral pieces in it are so splendid: the first sunrise after the Norn scene, with Siegfried's Hero motive and Brünnhilde's Love motive, which continues, becoming ever more triumphant, until the sound of Siegfried's theme rises up victoriously in *ff*. Then Siegfried's Rhine journey, his shattering Funeral March and the various interludes. The early awakening sunrise made the greatest impression on me, with the following scene between Siegfried and Brünnhilde, then the vanquishing of Brünnhilde by Siegfried in the form of Gunther, the scene with Siegfried and the Rhine maidens, Siegfried's death and funeral march, and finally, the titanically powerful, weightily pressing closing themes of Brünnhilde with the grandiose, heart-rending motive of Redemption through Love; the end of the work strikes me as something so utterly overpowering that I always begin to play this music with profound trembling; I am quite unworthy to play such music.

This performance took place on Palm Sunday 1902; during Easter week Webern had a second impressive musical experience in the form of Liszt's oratorio *Christus*, performed by the Vienna Choral Society (Singverein), an organisation whose regular conductor he was to become a quarter of a century later. This he also found to be 'a work of sublime beauty'.

> Now I am even more enthusiastic about Liszt, and to me it seems ideal to spread the music of this great master to the people, and to obtain for him the general recognition which, curiously enough, has so far not been given him. The blood rises to my head if I hear it said that Liszt possessed no invention, that he only understood how to orchestrate skilfully. The devil! Just take, for example, the March of the three holy kings from this oratorio – God, what supremely glorious melody blossoms forth there – or consider the absolutely incomparable 'Beatitudes'. With absolutely incomparable genius Liszt has woven the elements of the old church music into his oratorio. The entire work glows with exalted Christian intensity and leaves a powerful impression.

The record of Webern's trip to Bayreuth really begins with a post-card written to his cousin Ernst on 24 March 1902, in which Webern informs his cousin delightedly of his parents' offer to send the two boys to Bayreuth for two evenings and asks him to look into the possibility of getting tickets from the Wagner Society in Graz. Although it has never been stated that the trip was intended as a reward for both young men, it is clear that it came at an important point in the life of Diez as well: a letter from Webern written 7 June 1902 is addressed 'Herrn Doctor Ernst Diez' and congratulates the recipient on his newly won distinction, adding 'Long live the doctor!'

Webern's official record of the trip, which took place in August of 1902, covers ten pages (pp. 30–9) of Nb1, by far the most space devoted to any single experience. But of course this was not a single experience: it was a multitude of experiences, all new and wonderful for the boy from Klagenfurt. Webern was at an important juncture in his life that summer. His years at lower school in a provincial town were over; he was on the threshold of university, life in Vienna and, though he did not yet know it, meeting the two people who were to be the greatest influences on his life: Wilhelmine Mörtl and Arnold Schoenberg. The account of his pilgrimage to Bayreuth provides a window into his mind at this important time. We see a provincial boy, essentially naïve, confronted by many new sensations; a young man of intemperate ardour embarrassingly exposed, and of equally immoderate scorn for any whose enthusiasm happens not to match his own; a romantic who is greatly moved by ideals but who finds much of reality unpalatable.

His account begins with the observation that he had been unable to sleep the night before setting out because of his excitement of anticipation. He describes the beauty of the country passed through on the way to Bavaria, then is enraptured by the arrival there: 'O glorious Bavaria! Here there is still life!' Everything about the country enchants him: the beer, the food, the people – even, it seems, the traffic. The trip took them from Passau to Regensburg, where they stayed the night and visited the cathedral – which he described as magnificent – to Nuremberg. He tells us that his heart beat ever more quickly the nearer they came to Bayreuth. And 'at last—at last' they arrived, joining 'the many, many people who had come from all over the world to lovely Bayreuth, in the middle of Germany, to experience the glory that the great Master offers them through his works'. The Festspielhaus is the Temple of the Holy Grail. When the performance begins – of Parsifal, appropriately – Webern is overcome. There are no words to describe such an experience: 'Before such beauty one can only sink to one's knees, silent and dumb, and pray. . . . The sound of the orchestra from the mystical depths is beyond all praise: free from every imperfection, pure, pleasing sound.' And not only the sound: he describes the scenery as magical. Everything, he says, is magnificent and will leave an indelible impression. (And, indeed, it did.)

After a visit to Villa Wahnfried on the following day, a performance of the Flying Dutchman was greeted with similar enthusiasm. The scenery, the drama, the chorus were picked out as especially magnificent. Singled out as particularly wonderful were the end of the first act and the chorus scene in the last act.

The dark side of Webern's Bayreuth experience was probably inevitable: commensurate with the intensity of his all-consuming religious ecstasy was his deep contempt for those who did not share it, and one supposes this would have included nearly everyone over thirty who was in attendance. There is no room in his Temple of Bayreuth for social intercourse. He takes the socialist view that expensive and fashionable clothing is inimical to artistic sensibility or serious appreciation. He is even offended by the 'laughing faces'. It would appear that men in patent leather shoes and expensive cravats are, simply because of their apparel, unable to understand the immensity of what they are given the privilege to observe. (One thinks of the familiar pictures of Wagner, in his fine leather boots, his silk cravats and his extravagant velvet hats.) The young Webern bemoans the ignorance and the rudeness of these people who reduce Bayreuth to a social occasion and thus in his eyes necessarily miss its significance. ('These people are as ill-mannered as a provincial audience.') They talk – and even laugh! – in the Festspielhaus, and they have hardly left the Temple when they begin chattering idly about each other's clothing, as if they had not just witnessed something that transports 'people like us' to another world entirely. Horror of horrors: Bayreuth has become fashionable.

But most of all, Webern was disgusted by the audacity of an audience that would applaud Wagner in his own Temple. One should not smile, or laugh, or talk, but especially one should not applaud. The presumptuousness of ordinary mortals in indicating that they have found pleasure in the performance of *Parsifal* seemed to him outrageous.

After the two performances the young men began their homeward journey, which took them through Nuremberg to Munich, where they stopped for a visit. Here we read the only reference to painting and theatre in the first two notebooks. In Munich they visited the Neue Pinakothek, the Schack Gallery and the Secession. In the first two Webern was very taken with a Segantini painting, *Alpenlandschaft*, Böcklin's *Spiel der Wellen* and a picture by Herterich which he does not name; he says that wonderful pictures hang in these two galleries. In the Secession he was confronted for the first time by an entire exhibition of modern art. In view of the direction his life was to take within a few years, and the amount of time and energy he would devote in later life to defending the art and artists of his own day against the Philistines, it is amusing to read of his disappointment with what he saw there: 'I stood gaping! None of these pictures made an outstanding impression on me.' He says weakly that perhaps he was too tired from the trip.

In the evening they went to the theatre, a modern building by Riemerschmied that Webern thought quite beautiful, to see Arthur Schnitzler's *Liebelei*, 'a piece that gets on one's nerves!'

Webern's disgust with the Bayreuth audiences and with the majority of pictures in the Munich galleries, as well as the raptures elicited by the operas themselves and by the Segantini landscape at the Neue Pinakothek, all expressed in his meticulous diary accounts of this trip, were typical of both his attitudes and the language in which he would continue to express them. He was never to suffer fools gladly, and this category included anyone whose tastes fell outside the German-Austrian tradition from Bach to Mahler (and later Schoenberg) or whose intensity of feeling or commitment to art seemed insufficient.

Webern's interest in poetry during these years is much more apparent than his interest in painting, at least partly, one supposes, because a poem can be copied into a notebook whereas a painting cannot. Also, of course, he was beginning to compose, and, though one cannot say whether his interest in poetry led him to compose songs or his desire to write songs led him to explore poetry, the facts were that he read and copied down a great deal of poetry, and after the two cello pieces of 1899 he wrote only songs. Aside from Mörike, whose poetry came to his attention through Hugo Wolf's settings, and Nietzsche, who was probably fascinating primarily for his philosophical ideas, the poets represented in the first two notebooks are all turn-of-the-century lyric poets: Ferdinand Avenarius, Hermann Ubell, Robert Graf, Richard Dehmel, Stefan George, Otto Julius Bierbaum, Karl Hauptmann and Gustav Falke. Dehmel and George are familiar to the English-speaking world, largely through settings of their poetry by

Schoenberg, as well as by a more mature Webern. But the reputation of the others is more restricted.

Ferdinand Avenarius (1856–1923) was Richard Wagner's nephew, the son of his younger half-sister, Cäcilie Geyer-Avenarius. In addition to writing poetry he compiled several anthologies. Hermann Ubell founded the Art History Society in Graz and co-edited the *Grazer Kunst* during some of the time that Ernst Diez lived in that city, later moving to Linz, where he was custodian/director of the upper Austrian Landesmuseum from 1903 to 1937. In 1900 he gave several lectures under the auspices of the Art History Society which Diez almost certainly attended. Otto Julius Bierbaum was a poet set by Richard Strauss; his poem 'Traum durch die Dämmerung', copied on page 3 of Nb1, is the text of the first of Strauss' Op. 29 songs.[5]

Webern wrote or sketched nine songs in the years 1899–1902. Four of these were on texts by Avenarius and two were on anonymous texts. The remaining three were settings of poems by Dehmel, Falke and Theodor Storm. In anticipation of a later taste for the rarefied mysticism of Hildegard Jone the young Webern favoured lyric poems rich in nature metaphors and romantic readings of natural phenomena. But the things he chose to copy into his notebooks also show a healthy youthful interest in Woman and ideas of love, particularly of the tragic variety. One short piece, dated January 1901 and identified only as 'Indisches Liedchen', runs as follows:

> O Fate, if you are merciful,
> Do not assign to me human birth once again.
> But if that, then not love, and if that,
> Then not for one whom I cannot attain. (p. 11)

And again, quoting a favourite poet, Gustav Falke: 'Happiness is longing; fulfilment is death' (p. 8). Neither of these sentiments, one supposes, reflected the young Webern's own personal experience.

His letters to Ernst Diez provide a more accurate reflection of his personal life at this time. In November of 1900 he refers to regular dancing lessons, and in February of 1902 he writes:

I enjoyed this year's Carnival very much. I went to three parties where I had a very good time and danced the whole night through. I am now very enthusiastic about waltzing. To dance to the *Fledermaus* Waltz is simply wonderful.

The first of these letters is much taken up with enthusiastic references to a fellow dancing student, Stanzi, about whom Webern admits to being 'quite crazy' and who is 'rather well-disposed' towards him as well. It is his great misfortune to have been caught by some of his teachers at a coffee house in the hour following his dancing lesson that very afternoon, the result being four hours' detention and – much worse! – a ban on his further attendance at dancing lessons (apparently his only contact with the bewitching Stanzi). These two letters also describe the limits of a romantic attachment between his cousin Ernst and another of his dancing-class acquaintances, Frieda Hibler, a match in which Webern appears to have been a moving force. In November of 1900 he advises his cousin of Frieda's interest in him and suggests that he should 'take her' (if he doesn't find her 'too chic'); sixteen months later he relays her request that her letters and photograph be returned to her forthwith. There is no word concerning the fate of Webern and Stanzi. There is however reference to a school friend in the first of these letters – the only one who has been immortalised in this way. On this occasion Webern tells his cousin that his friend Supersperg (clearly a mutual friend) is his fellow sufferer in the coffee-house-banned-dancing-lessons affair. A year and a half later Supersperg is mentioned again, when his congratulations are added to Webern's own on the occasion of Diez's successful doctorate.

It was to his cousin Ernst that Webern confided his doubts and his concerns about the future. On 22 July 1901 he wrote of the dilemma that he would face in the following year when he had finished with the Gymnasium. His father naturally hoped that his only son would prepare himself to maintain the family estate, the most obvious way being to pursue a course of study at the College of Agriculture and then take up residence at the Preglhof. The prospect of doing this filled Webern with horror.

Webern had not kept his ambitions from his father, but the latter, who always appears as a reasonable and loving – even indulgent – parent, not only wished to see his son comfortably settled and the family property preserved, but was doubtful that the boy's talent was sufficient to ensure his success in a life of music. (It seems likely that the elder Webern recognised in his son the instability that was to make the whole of his life a precarious existence; in a father's terms one can only see his advice as sound.) The doubts about his musical abilities seem to have infected Webern himself – at least so he tells his cousin Ernst. He is determined, nevertheless, and in this letter he asks his cousin, who was already in university and thus presumably conversant with the ways of universities, to find out for him how one should proceed if one wished to become a conductor: what sort of study was required, and what sort of experience, how the important conductors of the day had prepared themselves. The letter ends, 'I don't know what to make of myself.' And in a letter of 8 December 1901, after showing enthusiasm for his cousin's most recent accomplishments at the piano, he despairs of his own success: 'God, if only I also could amount to something! But I have such small hands and also my memory is so weak that to memorise is difficult. This causes me a great deal of worry and grief.'

Notwithstanding the 'worry and grief' connected with his difficulties in playing the piano, it is clear that Webern was taking composition seriously by this time. Page 65 of Nb2 contains the following list:

Op. 1 4 Lieder

1. 'Vorfrühling'   (F. Avenarius: *Stimmen und Bilder*)
   E♭ Major
2. 'Wolkennacht'
   D♭ ['Major' written over 'minor']
3. 'Tief von Fern'   (R. Dehmel)
   E Major
4. 'Wehmut'   (F. Avenarius: *Stimmen und Bilder*)
   B Major
5. 'Fromm'   E♭ Major   (G. Falke)

The first four entries are written in ink, the last in pencil, and they clearly represent his thoughts on two separate – and, as it turns out, rather widely spaced – occasions. The first four songs, three of them on poems of Avenarius, were composed between the autumn of 1899 ('Vorfrühling'), when Webern was fifteen, and 15 July 1901 (the date on 'Wehmut'). It would seem that the original notebook entry was made in the late summer or autumn of 1901. Webern had written nothing more by the end of that year: on 8 December he complains to his cousin that his attempts at composition are coming to nothing, as he 'sadly cannot get anything together'. Nor, indeed, did he succeed in finishing anything until the end of the following summer, when he finally wrote the song 'Fromm', on a text by Gustav Falke. It must have been at this time that he returned to his list of Op. 1 songs and added the fifth song, thereby creating the contradiction between title ('4 Lieder') and list. 'Fromm' was written at the Preglhof and is dated 11 September 1902, at the end of Webern's last summer holiday before his entrance to university in Vienna, so it represents for him the end of an era – the last music composed before his formal theoretical instruction in music began. All five of these songs survive, though the second exists only in pencil sketches. None was considered worthy of publication by Webern, who subsequently designated his Passacaglia for orchestra, written during his years with Schoenberg, as his Op. 1.[6]

On page 29 of Nb1 Webern jubilantly announces his successful completion of the Gymnasium. The entry reads:

> On the morning of 11 July 1902
> Matura[7] fortunately achieved.
>
> Hurrah!

Free at last!
Here's to long life and the future.

Up to his entry to university Webern had very little exposure to music written by non-Germanic composers. This was the result of his growing up in rural Austria, where other traditions made few inroads.

Thus the style of his youthful compositions naturally has its roots in the German/Austrian tradition; the pieces written in 1899–1902 are chromatic – not atonal – with the harmonic motion taking unexpected directions that are very often inexplicable and unsatisfying. All are written with key signatures, though the shorter of the cello pieces shows already an uncomfortable relationship with its key signature, and this unease becomes more pronounced in the pieces written in the next few years. These and subsequent compositions prior to Webern's entrance into university in 1902 (eight additional works from these years survive, all songs with piano accompaniment) exhibit the same rich textures and occasionally adventurous but frequently awkward harmonic language.

Webern also tried his hand at writing poetry about this time. The second notebook contains five original poems (on pp. 72–6) which must date from either the summer or the autumn of 1902. The style of these is similar to that of the lyric poetry of Avenarius and others whose work appears elsewhere in the notebooks. The third of the poems is personal: it is entitled 'An den Preglhof' and is a nostalgic memory of the far away and beloved family estate (in which it was probably written). The first four poems are translated by Molden-hauer (HM: 65–6). The fifth, 'Traum', he did not translate, perhaps because he couldn't read it (the writing is extremely erratic and illegible in places), but more likely because it did not fit the picture of the young Webern that he was anxious to project. Unfortunately its illegibility prevents me from reproducing it as well, but enough of it is readable to tell that, unlike the others, it is gently erotic.

2   1902–8   Shaping forces

As far as I am concerned, there is nothing in the world about which I
did not learn something from you.
                    Webern, in a letter to Schoenberg, 2 September 1907

No one could have known how momentous the events of the next few
years would be for Webern. Matriculation at university is an important
passage in any young life; in Webern's case it was less influential than
were various other opportunities and relationships that came about as
the result of his move to the capital city. It was in Vienna, in the years
1902–6, that he met most of the people who would prove to be his closest lifelong friends: Heinrich Jalowetz, a fellow student at the university, Arnold Schoenberg and Alban Berg, to name only a few. It was
here that he saw both Richard Strauss and Gustav Mahler conduct for
the first time, in 1903, and, later, spent a memorable evening in the
company of the latter. And it was here that the Passacaglia, the work
which he finally gave the distinction of being his Op. 1, was written in
the spring of 1908 and given its first performance on 4 November of
the same year, with Webern conducting – almost certainly his first
appearance as a conductor in Vienna.

   Webern described his first year at university in letters to his cousin
Ernst.[1] They describe more or less the thoughts and reactions one
would expect from any young person entering university, particularly
a young person from the provinces who was being newly exposed to

26

the wonders and sophistication of a great capital. At first he is intimidated by the older and more experienced students and their worldly
attitudes. He is amazed at the amount of work required of him. He is
pleased about most of his teachers, uncertain about a few (he does
not attend the lectures of Diez [sic] who is reputed to 'have a speech
defect' and to be an anti-Wagnerian), but all in all he is pleased with
what he is doing: lessons on the piano and cello, lectures in early
music by Richard Wallaschek and in philosophy by Laurenz Müllner,
studies in harmony with Hermann Graedener and counterpoint with
Karl Navratil, and historical musicology with Guido Adler.[2] His cello
teacher is the solo cellist of the Konzertvereinsorchester, and his
piano teacher a young American woman who had studied with
Leschetizky.[3] According to Institute records he elected in future
years, besides his studies in music, to attend a large number of
courses in philosophy, a few in art history and one in the Catholic
liturgy. Two of the courses listed would seem to be particularly
significant: one entitled 'Albrecht Dürer and his time', and one entitled 'Nationalism'. He tells his cousin that when he first came to the
Institute he would have liked nothing more than to give it all up, but
by November it is clear that his confidence has increased and he feels
at home as a student. He has joined the Wagner Society, where he will
come into personal contact with well-known conductors and other
musicians. Furthermore his family has purchased a grand piano with
English action and a very nice tone ('a black piano', he tells his
cousin) with which he is quite pleased. On 18 February 1903 he
reports that his edition of a *Sacris solemnis* by Johannes Brassart (he
admits to not knowing to what century this piece belongs – perhaps
an early indication that musicology is not his real calling) is to appear
in the *Denkmäler der Tonkunst in Österreich*. This is after only a few
months' study, and he admits that this has been a great boost to his
self-confidence.[4]

There is one aspect of his descriptions of his new life that, in the
light of future events, one finds slightly disquieting. This is his
repeated reference to Jews. On 5 November he describes his class at

the Institute as including 'seven Jews, a Jewess, four Poles and four Germans'[5] and goes on to single out the Jews as 'so unfriendly etc'. Later, on 28 December, he remarks on the worldliness and presumption of the young people in Vienna. 'Every Jewish girl dares to judge the greatest artists . . . A Jewish boy who stood behind me in the queue not long ago had been there [to the Opera] thirty times already!' It would be wrong to infer from these youthful remarks that the mature Webern was antisemitic. His activities in the 1930s and 40s make it perfectly clear that he was not. But these youthful remarks are disturbing none the less.

When Webern came to Vienna in the autumn of 1902 he was far from inexperienced (he had, as we have seen, thought about and heard a quite respectable body of music), but his experience was that to be gained in a provincial town, and was thus necessarily restricted in various ways. While he had played an active part in the musical life of Klagenfurt, he had not had easy access to, for example, any of the great art museums or theatres, or to the opera. This probably explains his rather bewildered response to the art galleries of Munich and his contempt for the Schnitzler play he saw there in the summer of 1902. His opera experiences could be counted on the fingers of one hand; until his trip to Bayreuth, they were annual events.

The limited nature of his previous opera experience in conjunction with his great enthusiasm for Wagner had made his trip to Bayreuth in August of 1902 a most unforgettable experience. When he went to Vienna one month later the Bayreuth experience continued to dominate his life for some time. On 5 November he writes at the end of a letter to his cousin:

> Do you think sometimes of Bayreuth?
> The most beautiful hours for me are those which I can devote to memories.
> Most of the scenes are still for me vivid memories and if I am completely undisturbed the sound also comes back to me.
> It was really wonderfully beautiful!
> I hope to make a second pilgrimage next year. [This did not happen.]

As one who had glimpsed the Truth at Bayreuth only a month earlier, he was appalled at what he beheld at the Vienna Opera. There were ample opportunities for comparison: the Vienna Opera produced *The Flying Dutchman, Meistersinger, Tannhäuser, Tristan and Isolde, Lohengrin, Rienzi* and the entire *Ring* cycle in the 1902–3 season, and while Webern does not record his reactions to all of these it is pretty likely that he would have seen them all. He did write about *Götterdämmerung, The Flying Dutchman* and *Meistersinger*, in three successive weeks in September (Nb1, pp. 40–5). He informs his cousin Ernst that the Opera in Vienna is nauseating, pompous, simply dreadful; performances are disgraceful. On 5 November he asks, 'Have you seen any Wagner since Bayreuth?', going on to lament that he never expected to find such a difference between performances at Bayreuth and those in Vienna. 'God knows I always imagined what magnificence I should experience here. What a disappointment!' He complains bitterly about the visible orchestra, which produces, instead of a 'beautiful . . . sound from the "mystical abyss"', 'a loud din that regularly covers the voices of a large men's chorus'; he complains about the 'dreadful' ensemble, about the scenery and about the lack of the correct sense of distance between stage and audience. In his notebook he complains about Schalk's conducting and says that only Schmedes (who sang Siegfried) did his part justice. 'Only now do I really understand what Bayreuth means. . . . The phrase "one hears it just as beautifully somewhere else, for example at the Vienna Opera, as at Bayreuth" is nonsense. There is not another Bayreuth. Sadly!' After seeing *The Flying Dutchman* he asks, 'Was that supposed to have been *The Dutchman*?!!!' and says 'it was scarcely recognisable as [the same work as] the *Dutchman* at Bayreuth. Dear heaven! Is there not a single critic in Vienna who will take exception to this sort of thing?'

In spite of his horror at the productions, however, he tells his cousin that he has been to see *Die Meistersinger* five times (every performance so far). He is ecstatic about the work, which he must have been hearing for the first time, though in light of his enthusiasm for Wagner it is unlikely that he was unfamiliar with the score. He writes:

'Ernst, this Meistersinger is so beautiful as to drive one mad!' Nearly five pages of Nb1 are devoted to this opera (pp. 41–5). He is especially impressed with the character of Hans Sachs, whom he describes, significantly, as 'this good German man'. A notebook entry dated only October, and made after he attended his second *Meistersinger*, states that Reichmann sang and played the role of Sachs wonderfully well though Schalk still fell very short of conducting the score as it should be done. On this occasion Webern mentions in passing that he has also seen Schalk conduct *Tannhaüser*, which, unlike *Meistersinger*, he did very well (p. 49).

By February his contempt for the Vienna Opera's productions of Wagner had begun to fade. On 21 February he saw a new production of *Tristan and Isolde*, again with Schmedes, who was singing the part of Tristan for the first time. 'Sadly he is not right for the part. His voice is not right, and his acting leaves much to be desired.' Webern still has Winkelmann's Tristan (the performance he had seen in Graz at Eastertime of 1901) in his mind. Anna Mildenburg as Isolde, on the other hand, he finds extraordinarily pleasing. And the scenery, which he describes in some detail, is marvellous. Finally, he writes that the opera was conducted by Mahler, who 'brought out all the beauties of the orchestral score to magnificent effect'. Webern was particularly impressed with Mahler's handling of the long crescendo in the Prelude (pp. 61–2).

Webern had by this time seen Mahler conduct on several occasions. The first was a triple bill at the Opera on 4 October when, following Mozart's *Zaïde* ('real Mozart, lovely and tender, as clear and simple as a bright summer's day') conducted by Bruno Walter, Mahler conducted Bizet's *Djamileh* ('music bathed in an oriental glow, chock full of inspired rhythms, the orchestration enchanting') and a ballet by J. Hellmesberger entitled *Harlekin als Elektriker* ('an idiocy of the first order'). On this occasion Webern describes Mahler, whom he was seeing for the first time. 'An artist! Long black hair, clean-shaven. Spectacles. How he leads the orchestra! He gets everything out of the score' (pp. 46–7). Webern's interest in Mahler had already, of course, been sparked by his acquaintance with the Second Symphony; his fascination with the older composer grew as he watched him conduct in Vienna.

Sometime later in October Webern saw performances of Gluck's *Orpheus and Euridice*. Orpheus was sung by Edyth Walker, whom he had already heard in concert in Klagenfurt. About her Orpheus, he writes (p. 49): 'One of the strongest impressions I have ever experienced. This Walker sang unbelievably beautifully. I really cannot believe that anyone else in the whole world sings such a beautifully clear Orpheus. And how superbly she acted!' Of the work he writes: 'Gluck's opera is ... colossal. This is grandiose music of unapproachable magnitude.' And, significantly: ' I place the work next to the most magnificent creations of Wagner and Beethoven.' This was the greatest praise the young Webern could offer.

Later, in November, Webern records the fact that he has seen at the Opera *Carmen*, *Pagliacci*, *Cavalleria rusticana*, Liszt's *Legende von der heiligen Elisabeth* and Wilhelm Kienzl's *Der Evangelimann*, all wretched performances, except for Schmedes' 'fantastic, stunning' portrayal of Mattias Freundlicher in *Evangelimann* and his thrilling Pagliacci. Regarding the latter: 'It was an unparalleled experience!' He also records having seen Otto Ludwig's *Erbförster* at the Burgtheater. This list of works comes at the end of a long entry (pp. 51–7) dated November 1902 which takes the form of an essay summarising the musical experiences of the month. He begins this entry by deploring the surfeit of concerts facing the Viennese at this time of year – numerous performers of every description, most presenting, as he says, miserable programmes – and what he sees as the probably inevitable desensitisation of the public, who can no longer tell good from bad. He goes on to enumerate some of his experiences: Beethoven's Seventh Symphony (which he was hearing for the first time) and Liszt's *Mazeppa*, both conducted with 'warmth and love' by Siegfried Wagner; an evening of Hugo Wolf ('His songs are so exquisitely beautiful'); a terrible concert by the Krill Quartet ('the quartet in Klagenfurt played better'); his first hearing of Cornelius' Overture to

The Barber of Baghdad; Röntgen playing Beethoven's Fourth Piano Concerto ('This is an artist! Röntgen plays not as he wishes, but as Beethoven wished – he does not play Beethoven, he lives it.'). Webern offers his own very romantic interpretation of the Andante movement of the Beethoven concerto, as 'a pleading wife (the piano) and a violent man (the orchestra). The wife pleads, the husband answers coldly – until finally the wife dies of woe – the movement ends completely softly.' Webern mentions further having heard two pieces from Berlioz's *Romeo and Juliet*: 'Love scene' and 'Queen Mab', described as 'two marvellous things, one full of warmth, the other magnificently orchestrated'. A separate entry preceding this essay (pp. 50–1) records his having heard Ferdinand Loewe conduct Mozart, Brahms and Beethoven (the Fifth Symphony) on 29 October.

The new year brought several important performances. On 19 January Weber's *Euryanthe* was performed at the Vienna Opera, with Mahler conducting and Berta Foerstrová-Lauterová as an unforgettable Euryanthe, and on 22 January Bizet's *Carmen*, with the title role played by Marie Gutheil-Schoder. Webern was much impressed by both and observed that Wagner owed a great deal to Weber. 'How like Wagner this drama is, or, better, how like Weber Wagner is. We find particularly already in *Euryanthe* the meaningful interaction of the various characters through a certain handling of motives, and progressions that are pregnant with expression' (pp. 57–8). To his cousin he writes: '*Euryanthe* is one of the greatest influences on Wagner. In many places it really looks exactly like a Wagner score. The music of *Euryanthe* is much more dramatic and more beautiful than that of *Freischütz*. The way the Philharmonic played the overture under Mahler is indescribable!' (18 February 1903).

On 25 January Webern heard one of his greatest loves, this time in its entirety. A carefully spaced page (p. 59) was devoted to recording this occasion:

> Today, the 25th of January 1903, I heard
> the Ninth Symphony of Beethoven.

The Philharmonic Orchestra.
Conductor: J. Hellmesberger.

Oh, divine Beethoven!

It was the holiest hour
of my life up to now!

In a letter to his cousin Ernst he writes: 'Even Bayreuth did not have such an effect on me as the last movement of the Ninth, in spite of J. Hellmesberger and the *poor* performance throughout' (18 February 1903).

Less than three weeks later, another Ninth was offered: Bruckner's, in its première performance under Ferdinand Loewe. (To his cousin Webern writes, on 18 February, 'I have heard two 9ths'.) He was ecstatic. In his notebook (p. 60) he wrote that 'The performance was magnificent. The work itself is of the greatest solemnity. Bruckner dedicated it to "dem lieben Gott", and with the Adagio took leave of the world.' To his cousin he wrote in very similar language, continuing,

> really, if you listen quite attentively, you can, at the end of the Adagio, which is wonderfully gentle and transfigured, imagine watching the dear man's ascent to Heaven, higher and higher, further and further, until with the last, softest, long, long held E-major chord of the tubas (five!) and horns Heaven is opened to him. There can scarcely be anything more beautiful than this Adagio. Of course both the other movements are also magnificent, especially the Scherzo, which sounds like a mighty dance of will-o'-the-wisps in a sinister swamp. At least an anchor is provided by the notes of the trumpets in this movement.

Following Bruckner's Ninth was his *Te Deum*. The result was 'extraordinary'.

In the same letter Webern reports having heard Felix Weingartner and the Vienna Orchestra perform Berlioz's *Symphonie fantastique* and Liszt's Dante Symphony. ('Both works are colossal.') This prompts him to remark once again that he places Liszt among the greatest composers: 'For me, the line from Beethoven continues through Liszt, Bruckner. Wagner, being a dramatist, stands completely apart.' He writes that he has also heard Bruckner's Fourth Symphony twice, once under Loewe and once under Felix Mottl, on which occasion the Venusberg music was also played. He goes on to describe an evening with Mottl: 'Mottl was with us in the Wagner Society on the evening before his concert, and he played the whole last act of Tristan for us on the piano, singing the parts of Tristan, Kurwenal, Brangäne, Isolde etc. It was amazing!'

On 22 February Hugo Wolf died, after several years of anguish. His death made a strong impression on the young Webern, who greatly admired his songs and had for many years expressed his admiration by copying the texts of his favourite Wolf songs into his notebooks. He attended the funeral at the Church of the Holy Redeemer, where Ferdinand Loewe conducted a Wolf song for mixed choir followed by the Adagio from Bruckner's Eighth Symphony (written as an elegy for Wagner). The notebook entry ends: 'Aeons cannot obliterate the traces of his days on earth.'

Another 'first' occurred on 4 March, when Webern saw Richard Strauss conduct the Berlin Tonkünstler Orchestra in a programme of Strauss, Liszt, Tchaikowsky and Bruneau. He described Strauss' own music as 'splendid, magnificent creations of great genius', but the Berlin orchestra as disappointing. He adds that the hall was empty.

Webern's notebooks become much less informative after the early spring of 1903. Entries for the 1902–3 and 1903–4 concert seasons are separated only by five pages in Nb1 on which ten poems by various authors have been copied. There is no record of Webern's activities during the summer of 1903, and concert descriptions for the 1903–4 season are much less copious than those in previous years.

The first notebook contains nine pages devoted to a series of eight Philharmonic concerts, and no record of any other events. The conductor is given in every case; the programme is listed until the last; there is commentary, often quite brief, until the seventh. The conductors were Ernst von Schuch,[6] W. J. Safanoff from Moscow, Arthur Nikisch and Dr Carl Muck from Berlin. Works mentioned were by Haydn, Handel, Beethoven (Fifth, Seventh and Eighth Symphonies), Glazunov, Scriabin, Rimsky-Korsakov (these three in the all-Russian programme conducted by Safanoff), Bach, Schmidt, Berlioz, Schumann, Brahms, Wagner, Mozart, Goldmark, Weber, Schubert and Bruckner (Seventh Symphony).[7] Among Webern's comments: he found the 'Jupiter' Symphony to be one of the greatest art works of all time; Brahms' Third Symphony 'cold and without particular inspiration, . . . badly orchestrated – grey on grey'; Wagner deeply passionate and powerful; Schubert's C Major Symphony sublimely radiant, jubilant, 'so genuinely Viennese'; the Weber *Konzertstuck* in F minor music that was no longer worth listening to; Schumann's Fourth Symphony boring;[8] Berlioz's *Roman Carnival* difficult but charming. Of the Russian music, significantly, he had real praise only for the Glazunov Symphony, which he found not particularly Russian. There is no commentary on the Bruckner Seventh. Surprisingly, in view of the predominance of opera in Webern's musical life the previous season, there is no mention of it in the 1903–4 season.

A series of five Bruckner concerts listed in Nb2 occurred in the 1903–4 season, in spite of their position before the list of the 1902–3 season at the Hofoper, and succeeding pages contain lists of offerings at various other venues as well – the Burgtheater and the Deutsches Volkstheater and Karltheater, where the appearance of 'Miss Isodora [*sic*] Duncan' on 21 March is written in very large letters and underlined (though there is no indication that Webern attended this evening).

In the late spring of 1904 Webern and his fellow student Heinrich Jalowetz travelled to Berlin to see Hans Pfitzner with the hope that he might take them on as pupils in composition. Pfitzner, who came from a family of musicians, had been trained at the Hoch Conservatory in Frankfurt and was known as both a conductor and a pianist. In 1904 he was a teacher at the Stern Conservatory and first Kapellmeister at the Theater des Westens in Berlin. Webern presumably knew Pfitzner's opera *Der arme Heinrich* (written in 1891–3): in a letter to his cousin dated 8 December 1901 he laments the fact that the theatre in Graz (where his cousin lived) appears to be bent on producing only second-rate operas that season, and asks,

> What kind of rubbish must this Boïto's *Mephistopheles* be then, or Zöllner's *Versunkene Glocke*? Why do they not do Kienzl's *Don Quixote* or Schillings' *Ingwelde* or *Der arme Heinrich* by Pfitzner, or the operas of A. Ritter?

According to Josef Polnauer, later a close friend of Webern, this meeting was terminated abruptly when Pfitzner spoke disparagingly of Strauss and Mahler. Webern responded by grabbing Jalowetz by the arm and leaving the room – and Berlin. Having been thus disappointed, Webern, in the autumn of 1904, made what was probably the most momentous move of his life. He sought out Arnold Schoenberg, a self-taught Viennese composer, himself only thirty years of age, who had advertised in the local newspapers for pupils in an attempt to keep body and soul together. According to Wildgans Webern may have gone to Schoenberg on the advice of Guido Adler, who frequently sent his most promising students to Schoenberg for study in composition.

Schoenberg was not an unknown quantity. Already in December of 1900 the performance of his music had caused dissension in Viennese music circles. Webern had heard *Verklärte Nacht*, Schoenberg's string sextet after a poem by Richard Dehmel, in the autumn of the previous year, and as early as 1902 he had seen and been fascinated by a score of Schoenberg's *Pelleas und Melisande* shown him by a friend. (He told Schoenberg much later, in a letter dated 2 September 1907, that ever since seeing the *Pelleas* score he had been 'driven by the desire to know how the music would sound', and that the impression made on him by *Verklärte Nacht* was 'one of the greatest [he] had ever experienced'.)

Schoenberg's only affiliation was an unofficial one with the Schwarzwald School, a private school run by the philanthropist Dr Eugenie Schwarzwald, who offered him the school's facilities for the teaching of courses in harmony and counterpoint. He would have been considered a risk, to say the least. But what no one could know then was the almost messianic attraction he was to have for his follow-ers in the years to come.

Webern was probably Schoenberg's first private pupil in Vienna. He was joined almost immediately by Karl Horwitz and Heinrich Jalowetz, with Alban Berg and Erwin Stein following very shortly. This nucleus of Schoenberg disciples was to remain faithful and close-knit; all gained prominence in their fields – composition, conducting, music publishing – and all were to remain lifelong friends. Egon Wellesz, another of Webern's colleagues at the university, joined the group the following autumn, by which time Schoenberg was no longer associated with the school and was teaching at his home.

Schoenberg must have had great personal magnetism: the depth of devotion shown by his original students over the course of several decades is difficult to understand in the light of surviving anecdotes and documents, in which he almost invariably appears to be a person of monumental arrogance and megalomania. Paul Amadeus Pisk, his pupil from 1917 to 1919, described him as tyrannical; Salka Viertel, the sister of the pianist Edward Steuermann, who studied with Busoni in Berlin and then with Schoenberg from 1912 to 1914, spoke of his egoism and said that he was 'like an octopus' with the young men around him (Smith: 99, 97). He seems to have had utter faith in the divine nature of his own talent: in 1927 he wrote 'I . . . stick to writing [my music] on orders from The Most High'.[9] It is embarrassing to read his students' immoderate expressions of adoration and self-flagellation in response to their master's terse and bad-tempered, and often mean, rebukes. This is especially true in the case of Berg, whose courtesy, patience and generosity seem never to have flagged in the face of the older man's constant fault-finding. Webern's subservience and self-abnegation were equal to Berg's, but for some reason he was always treated more respectfully by Schoenberg: as the years passed Schoenberg wrote to Webern as an equal while Berg was always treated as a child, remaining until his death the object of irritation and annoyance and the subject of humiliation. Possibly Schoenberg felt closer to Webern – and felt him to be less of a threat – because throughout his life Webern suffered a public rejection like that on which his teacher thrived and made his reputation, while Berg enjoyed the occasional success. But this cannot explain Schoenberg's feelings towards the two men at the beginning of their relationship. One is tempted to see the differences in Schoenberg's attitude towards the two students in basic and rather unflattering terms. A thumbnail description of Schoenberg at this time would show a self-made man of very slight stature, no particular physical attraction and an abrasive personality, who had no social position, no money and few friends, and who abhorred – or, defensively, claimed to abhor – society. He must have been intimidated by the tall and physically handsome Berg, as well as envious of the sophistication that came so easily to him. Berg was universally described by those who knew him as possessing a natural nobility and gentleness. Webern, on the other hand, was, like Schoenberg, physically diminutive, and with his provincial background and his nervous disposition, which manifested itself in the expression of alternately unbridled enthusiasm and intemperate rage, he must have experienced the same social unease as Schoenberg. Perhaps it is not surprising that Schoenberg felt more sympathy for Webern, insulting Berg whenever possible.

In any case, when Webern associated himself with Schoenberg in 1904 he was doing much more than simply choosing a teacher of composition. He was, probably unconsciously, setting the course of the rest of his life by declaring himself in the ranks of Vienna's musical pariahs and attaching himself to one of history's most demanding and unforgiving masters. It is curious that this meeting, which clearly was of such significance for him, was not recorded anywhere, either in his notebooks or in his correspondence with his cousin. The second notebook ends after the lists of concert and theatre offerings of the 1902–3 season, and the first is very sketchy after March of 1904 (there is for example also no mention of the visit to Pfitzner, which must have occurred about that time). The last dated entry in this notebook (p. 106) was made at Christmastime 1906, two years after the entry of Schoenberg into Webern's life, yet the name of Schoenberg is nowhere mentioned. There are some fourteen pages after this entry, but they are blank except for a short credo on page 119: 'Through our deep and profound love we will become complete human beings who live only inwardly and who cultivate and protect their souls.'

A third notebook is specially devoted to a trip taken at Whitsun of 1905. After that either Webern gave up his habit of keeping a diary until 1913, or the books in which he did so have not survived. There are also no letters to his cousin extant from the time between February 1903 and July 1908. According to Moldenhauer (HM: 48) Webern had, in 1902, met (not for the first time) and fallen in love with Wilhelmine Mörtl, his first cousin (their mothers were sisters), his future wife and as far as anyone knows the only woman with whom he was ever in love. Moldenhauer's account seems to have been based on an entry at the end of page 28 of Nb1 (earlier on this page are the end of the commentary on Liszt's *Christus*, which was heard in Vienna during Easter Week of that year, on the visit whose primary purpose was to attend *Götterdämmerung*, and the announcement of Carl von Webern's promotion to the Ministry in Vienna, dated May 1902). This is a personal reflection dated 'Pfingsten,[10] 1902, am Pregelhof [sic]':

> Though the trees are in bloom it doesn't feel much like spring. It rains constantly – – And yet I am so happy. Everything produces a sweet nostalgia in me, an indescribably sweet nostalgia. Such dear, [. . .][11] pictures come to my mind, always as if a beloved, sweet countenance greets me from far, far away.

There is no mention either of Wilhelmine or of a meeting, nor indeed of a visit to her family, but Moldenhauer's explanation seems likely, as the Mörtls lived in Vienna, where Wilhelmine's father was a notary. On the other hand it is possible that Webern's dreamy springtime mood might have been more general in nature and not associated with a particular person. In any case the notebook does supply concrete evidence of a further and conclusive encounter three years later, in the form of the diary of a five-day walking trip the two young people took together in May of 1905.

This is the enraptured and poetic outpouring of a young man who is in love with both the young woman at his side and the country that surrounds them. The images and the language emulate those of the lyric poets that he has read with such ardour in recent years. The account is written in pencil and the handwriting is extremely difficult to read. The young couple began by taking the train to Rosenburg, a village about sixty-five kilometres to the northwest of Vienna where there was a castle, then walked over 'awakening fields' to an old Benedictine monastery at Altenburg for lunch, then through forests and fields and meadows, over hills, through quiet villages, past dreaming mills, to Zwettl for the first night. A lark, a rainbow, meadow flowers, blue skies, sunshine, the wondrous beauty of spring – these are the components of the account. The last page is devoted to a description of the meadow flowers in their myriad colours – 'white, gold, blue, red' – presaging an older Webern who would never record a trip into the mountains without describing in detail the alpine flowers he had found there.

The account of the trip ends with the complete text of the second of Wolf's *Songs of a Wayfarer*, a joyous May song which continues seamlessly the idyll of the preceding pages (pp. 86–7). The following three pages are devoted also to poetry, and on page 91 is an entry similar in spirit to the one of Pfingsten 1902 quoted above. This one is headed '10 July 1905' and marks the end of a year (an academic one, presumably):

Now again a year has ended.
It has brought me many and meaningful experiences.
I have found my happiness – –
All joys and all pain that I suffered radiate over me in the light of our
    love – – –
Now I am separated from her.
In the solitude of forests and mountains am I and my
Soul longs for her, for her love.

O, if the wings of my longing could carry my love to her.

How painful is parting!

The next few pages contain notes on a book about the harmony of the spheres, some calculations of expenses and what appears to be lecture notes about the Mass and other liturgical music; there is no date on any of these pages, but they are very likely from 1905, as Webern attended the course in Catholic liturgy in the summer term of that year. After this the notebook resumes its function (briefly) as a diary of observations on music and art, but the dates are 6 November 1904 and 3 February 1905. The next – and last – date in this book is 'Christmas 1906', the heading on page 106.

In the summer of 1905 Webern travelled again to Munich, this time alone, and this time with his loved one much in his thoughts. The third of his notebooks is a diary, written for 'meine Wilhelmine', of this trip, which was a long one, lasting from 29 July to 6 September. This whole book is in pencil and once again the handwriting is extremely untidy. There are many emendations. In some cases original text has been scribbled out or a line has been drawn through it and replacement text written above or after or in the margin, in other cases new text has simply been written heavily over the original (a technique often used later in the sketchbooks); both situations are difficult to decipher now. The notebook consists of twenty-eight pages of writing; there are several blank pages at both the beginning and the end.

The account begins with a long description of Salzburg, with which Webern was enchanted.

> Never in my life have I seen a town that is so at one with its surroundings as Salzburg. The style of the Salzburger farmhouse is the same as the style of the Salzburger townhouse. The houses are nearly all built in the same way, very high—3–4 stories, all white with oblique roofs and gables. The streets extremely narrow and crooked. It is the organic unity of the town that makes such a magnificent impression.

> From afar the appearance of the fortress, 'Hoher Salzburg', and the surrounding country is indescribably beautiful. I arose early in the morning on a wonderfully beautiful sunny day. Up there it was fragrant and sweet, with all the castle's interwoven memories of

times past; the town in bright sunlight on both sides of the blue
Salzach; and the scenic location of this town!: on one side the mighty,
towering mountains, on the other the vast expanse of the Bavarian
plateau, where the eyes can roam over endless distances. As I was
thus absorbed in the sight of this beauty, the bells sounded, playing
from the tower in the town—light, sweet ringing getting lost in
sunny space—and soon afterwards the centuries-old barrel organ
rang out in the fortress itself, intoning a splendid chorale . . . in such
moments I feel God in my soul.

He goes on to describe the Mozart house and Mozarteum, and the
house of Paracelsus, and ends with the observation that 'there are
many other monuments of German culture in this beautiful city as
well'.

Then he revisits Munich, where his reactions are different from
those of his earlier trip, only two years before. He first writes about
the Alte Pinakothek, where he mentions particularly the wonderful
'romantic artists' Raphael, Coreggio and Tintoretto, the prints of
Rembrandt, Hals and Ruysdael, and 'the other pictures of the masters
. . . the Adoration of Christ, altar pictures and pictures of the apostles
and other works from the same time'. But none of these could match,
for him, the wonderful portraits by Dürer. And of these one stood out
above all the rest: a self-portrait, which he described characteristically
as 'the most sublime countenance that I have ever seen . . . the most
wonderful image of German man'.

A return visit to the Neue Pinakothek and the Schack Gallery elicits
a more studied response than it did in 1902, though the focus has not
changed: he is still most impressed by Schwind, Böcklin and
Segantini. In the 'hideous Glaspalast' he finds 'whole rooms full of
the most dreadful pictures from which one flees in horror', though he
finds three pictures worth mentioning: a fresco by Fritz Hodler, a portrait by Albert Welti and *Der Fremdling* by Fritz Erler. In the Neue
Pinakothek he 'found exactly the same thing . . . One painting by
Böcklin, *Spiel der Wellen*, one each by Hartung, Kalckreuth, Schwind,
Segantini, and that was all. Everything else mediocre or complete rub-

bish.' In the Schack Gallery, 'Here again, more disappointments . . . The most marvellous works of art hanging alongside the ugliest dreck. Of the Böcklins, I was particularly taken with the *Ideale Frühlingslandschaft*; the *Villa am Meer* is beautiful and *Die Seeschlange* is quite wonderful, perhaps my favourite Böcklin to date . . .' But most of all he liked Schwind, and especially *Des Knaben Wunderhorn*, which he describes at great length. 'One cannot imagine anything lovelier than this picture.'

He also visited the Prince Regent Theatre, for a performance of *Die Meistersinger*. He describes the theatre, which is modelled on Bayreuth and pleases him very much. He complains however that in this case having the orchestra 'sunken and concealed' does not succeed in producing the distinction between voices and orchestra that was Wagner's ideal: 'very often the one tone colour is blurred with the other; either one hears too little orchestra or the singing is completely drowned out. Also the sound of the brass is so strong that there is scarcely ever a *piano* to be heard.' And he found the performance unsatisfactory in other ways as well: the director, Arthur Nikisch, took all the tempos 'unbelievably fast', with the result that the 'violins lacked the sublime repose and serenity, the solemnity that is necessary'. On the plus side were the scenery, which was declared to be very beautiful, and Fritz Heinhals' Hans Sachs, though 'all the other portrayals were mediocre; that of Walther simply absurd.' The orchestra played well on the whole but bore no comparison with the orchestra of the Vienna Opera. Finally, an admission: 'I have learned one thing: . . . it has been made clear to me that we are closer to Bayreuth than these people of Munich'(!).

There are only two entries in Nb1 (and none in Nb2) from the 1904–5 season. Both are lengthy and interesting. The first, dated 6 November 1904, was sparked by a concert in which a Mozart symphony, Pfitzner's Scherzo in C minor and the 'Eroica' were played under Felix Mottl. Webern at first writes that because of circumstances (on which he does not elaborate) he was not able to enjoy the concert as he had hoped to, but that in any case the magnificent

Vienna orchestra left nothing more to be said. He did however have
something to say about the 'Eroica' itself, which was clearly a work for
which he felt a deep affinity. His often-quoted remarks bring together
several important facets of his maturing aesthetic: his unshakeable
reverence for Beethoven; his strong liking for the pictures of
Segantini; his romantic engagement with ideas of genius, purity,
truth, divinity; his proclivity for solitude; and perhaps above all his
deep feeling for the mountains, their strength and their beauty.

> From sadness and pain . . . . . TRUTH.

> The genius of Beethoven reveals itself more and more clearly to me. It
> gives me a higher power, knowledge, knowledge in the end when one
> veil after another is torn away, and his genius shines for me ever more
> radiantly – and one day the moment will come when I am directly
> imbued, in brightest purity, with his divinity. He is the comfort of
> my soul, which searches and cries after truth.

> I yearn for an artist in music such as Segantini was in painting, whose
> music would have to be what a man writes in solitude, far from all the
> bustle of the world, in the sight of glaciers, of eternal ice and snow, of
> the dark mountain giants, so it would be like Segantini's pictures. The
> breaking of an alpine storm, the power of the mountains, the radiance
> of the summer sun on flower-strewn meadows, all these would have
> to be in the music, a spontaneous birth from alpine solitude.

The only other notebook entry from this season records an experience
that was in its way just as profound for the young student. The date is 3
(or 4, the number is illegible) February 1905, and the entry records a
concert of Mahler songs. Webern admits to no great liking for those
on Rückert texts. He finds them too sentimental and opines that
Mahler's occasional lapses into sentimentality, which he says go
against the 'great and sincere' personality of the man himself, can
perhaps be explained by his Jewishness. But other things about the
songs are very much to his liking.

> What I wonder at in all the songs is the great expressiveness of his
> vocal parts – this is of an overwhelming intensity. I think especially of

the fourth of the *Kindertotenlieder* ('oft denk' ich, sie sind nur
ausgegangen') or 'Ich atmet' einen linden Düft'.

The important event of the evening however was a gathering of
Mahler's friends and guests afterwards to which Webern was invited.
Here he

> had the opportunity to get to know more about the personality of
> Gustav Mahler. These hours spent in his presence will always remain
> with me as an exceedingly happy memory, since it was the first time
> that I experienced the direct influence of a really great personality.

There was a discussion of Rückert's lyric poetry and of the *Wunderhorn*
texts, some of which Mahler said he did not understand. Then the talk
turned to counterpoint.

> Schoenberg said that only Germans could write counterpoint.
> Mahler pointed out the old French composers, Rameau, and so
> on, and allowed that among the Germans only Bach, Brahms and
> Wagner were great contrapuntalists. 'Nature is the model for us in
> these things. Just as in nature the whole universe has developed from
> the primordial cell, from plants, animals, and men on to God, the
> Supreme Being, so also in music a larger structure should develop
> from a single motive, in which is contained the germ of everything
> that is yet to be.' In Beethoven one nearly always finds a new motive
> in the development. The whole development should, however,
> challenge a single motive; in this sense even Beethoven cannot be
> considered a great contrapuntalist. Variation should be the most
> important factor in a musical work. A theme would have to be really
> exceptionally beautiful, like one of Schubert's, for its unvaried return
> to be found pleasing. For him, Mozart's string quartets were over at
> the first double bar. The task of modern creative composers is to
> combine the contrapuntal skill of Bach with the musical idiom of
> Haydn and Mozart.

At this point the notebooks stop giving us an insight into Webern's
response to the music and the people with whom he came into contact.
Probably now that he was a part of the Schoenberg circle and had close

friends of like mind with whom to discuss things the place for the expression of his ideas moved from paper to speech, from isolation to collegiality. Thus the lack of diaries should perhaps be seen as a healthy sign. It is also possible, of course, that there were more diaries.

At the end of June 1906 Webern received his doctorate from the university for his thesis, an edition of the *Choralis Constantinus* of Heinrich Isaac. There was some difficulty, as Wickhof, the art historian with whom Webern had enrolled for three courses during his years at university and who was initially assigned as his second reader, refused to act in this capacity; according to Antonicek he struck his name out vigorously on the dissertation. A third reader, Friedrich Jodl, was subsequently called upon, and the work was passed with a positive report signed by Adler and Jodl.[12] It must have pleased Webern to have completed the degree, though by this time his university studies had taken second place to his compositional studies and the related activities of the Schoenberg circle.

Webern's composing had been suffering a lull at the time that he moved to Vienna in 1902 and began his university study. Only one composition dates from 1902, the song 'Fromm', written in September at the Preglhof, just before the move to Vienna. Once established in Vienna, however, he began composing again, presumably as a part of his studies, since he now began to write, in addition to songs, music for string quartet, for piano and for string orchestra. Key signatures disappear for the first time in some of the songs from 1903; though this does not indicate the absence of tonality, the more adventurous pieces do not begin and end in the same key. There is little harmonic progression in the traditional sense in the early pieces and the level of dissonance is in most cases rather high, but the basic harmonic language remains emphatically triadic. Phrases and movements inevitably end on pure triads, though harmonic motion between these cadence points is unpredictable. Textures are thick and a wide range is covered, with extended measured arpeggios, low bass tremolos and movement in octaves, both open and filled in with thirds or triads.

A work for large orchestra, written in 1904 just before Webern went to Schoenberg, is in a tonal idiom that is quite different from that of the songs of the previous years and offers tantalising speculation about the direction Webern's composition might have taken had he in fact studied with someone other than Schoenberg.[13] Im *Sommerwind* is a luxuriant and evocative rhapsody, nearly fifteen minutes in length, in the style of Richard Strauss. After this optimistic youthful essay this style disappears forever.

The influence of Schoenberg begins to be felt in the work done the following year. For the first time there are no songs, and Webern concentrates on music for string quartet. Five pieces survive – a set of orchestral variations, three movements for string quartet and one for piano quintet; Webern continued to write almost exclusively for string quartet and orchestra for the next two years. In two of the movements for string quartet, both written between June and August of 1905, we see a composer of considerably greater refinement and sophistication than the youth of even one year earlier. Perhaps the most striking difference between these and earlier pieces is in their coherence, and in the logic, both structural and harmonic, that governs them. Whereas in the earlier pieces the unexpected was simply startling, and often confusing and disappointing as well, now it is a pleasure: because here motion is directed, the surprise serves only to interrupt, not to deflect or dissipate. The first of these movements, and the shorter and more lighthearted, is known as *Langsamer Satz*. It is Brahmsian in style and texture, with sumptuous harmonies, is simple but secure structurally, and is altogether an agreeable piece in a late romantic style. The longer piece (in fact the longest instrumental movement in all of Webern's music), known simply as String Quartet, shows an interesting convergence of influences. During the 1903–4 concert season Webern had heard Schoenberg's sextet for strings, *Verklärte Nacht*, and been profoundly impressed. The 1905 String Quartet is Webern's *Verklärte Nacht*: the influence of Schoenberg's work expresses itself in many ways. But there are also other influences. Webern noted on his sketches for the quartet that it was inspired by Segantini's triptych *Werden–Sein–Vergehen* (Becoming–Being–Passing away); in addition the opening and various transitions within the work are obviously modelled on the 'Muß es sein?' of Beethoven's Quartet Op. 135. In view of the notebook entry of 6 November 1904 quoted earlier (see p. 44), in which Webern couples Beethoven and Segantini, it is clear that the conjunction of references associated with this work was not a coincidence. Finally, and perhaps quite by chance (but who can say?), the motive that is used as a unifying device throughout this movement – Webern's 'Muß es sein?' – is the three-note cell that was to be the all-important germ motive in his twelve-note Op. 24 Concerto over a quarter of a century later.

In 1906 Wilhelmine Mörtl was sent to Geneva for the summer. After finishing university Webern again spent the summer at the Preglhof with his family. There he busied himself with composition exercises set by Schoenberg, a series of eighteen chorale harmonisations. No longer distracted by university studies he produced a large number of sketches in the remainder of this year, all for instrumental movements, and mostly uncompleted. None has the assurance of the 1905 String Quartet.

In the early autumn Webern returned to Vienna, to study with Schoenberg and to do some occasional menial work at the Volksoper, where Alexander Zemlinsky, Schoenberg's brother-in-law, was first conductor. It surely would have been expected that Webern should take up a conducting post upon leaving the university, but by this time he had become so dependent on Schoenberg that to leave Vienna was unthinkable.

Webern had scarcely returned to the city in September 1906 when he was called back to the Preglhof by a crisis in the health of his mother, who was a diabetic. Aged only fifty-three, she was dead when he arrived there, on 7 September. Webern was greatly affected by her death. He makes repeated references to it in the following years, and the Six Pieces for Large Orchestra, Op. 6, written in 1909, were an attempt to express this experience in music. In writing to Schoenberg about these pieces just before their first performance in 1913, Webern described his intentions at length.

There are not many records of the subsequent year and a half of Webern's life until he left Schoenberg's tutelage and took up his first conducting position in the summer of 1908. The last two works written while he was studying with Schoenberg, and the first two Webern felt to be worthy of opus numbers, were the Passacaglia for orchestra and the chorus *Entflieht auf leichten Kähnen* on a text by Stefan George. The Passacaglia, staunchly in D minor, is formally the most rigorous work so far, though its inevitable repetitions are well masked by a superstructure of larger sections and by frequent variations in tempo and texture. The influence of Brahms seems evident. The choral work, much less well known, is perhaps of more importance as a forecast of what was to come in later years: it is here that Webern for the first time uses canon on a large scale.

It is impossible to say, though interesting to speculate, exactly how Webern's association with Schoenberg changed the course of his life. Certainly the impact of Schoenberg's personality and ideas on at least his first set of students, and most particularly on Webern and Berg, was inordinate. Schoenberg's opinions and attitudes were absolute and allowed for neither opposition nor adjustment. And it must be said that his focus was very narrow. His notions of developing variation and counterpoint derived from an almost exclusively German/ Austrian repertoire of instrumental 'absolute' music, and he saw very little of any value outside this canon. He had little or no time for descriptive or programme music (in spite of his early *Pelleas und Melisande* and *Verklärte Nacht*, both written after texts, by Maurice Maeterlinck and Richard Dehmel) or for the 'nationalist' music that was a popular idiom around the turn of the century.[14] And, though he was to write several stage works and an opera himself, theatre music was not a genre to which he gave any attention in his teaching or prose writing, except on occasion to point out that the all-important elements of classically structured music did not function in this case. Some of his particular dogmas matched those that were already developing in the young Webern, and in these cases Schoenberg's intractability simply served to reinforce what was already there in a nascent form. His veneration of Beethoven is an example: we have seen the overpowering esteem for this master as something already well developed in the young Webern several years before he met Schoenberg. But this agreement of proclivities was not absolute. Schoenberg was, for example, a Brahmsian, and it is surely no coincidence that from 1905 onwards Webern says nothing more about Wagner, whose music he adored immoderately up to that time – in whose music he had in fact invested a considerable amount of time, energy and thought. And what of his great admiration, expressed earlier, for the operas of Weber and Gluck, or the dramatic works of Liszt? These names no longer figure after the autumn of 1904. Those who studied composition with Webern in the 1930s and 40s have reported his complete disdain for the music of all other national cultures, recalling his insistence that the music of Berlioz, Elgar and Tchaikovsky was only a 'pale reflection' of the 'real' music of Austria and Germany. This from the man who thirty years earlier had found the *Symphonie fantastique* 'colossal' and the *Roman Carnival* 'charming'. Who can say to what extent Schoenberg was responsible for this narrowing of vision?

Schoenberg's musical xenophobia (see the opinion recorded by Webern during the Mahler evening, that only Germans could write counterpoint, and his almost complete reliance on examples from German music in his teaching and his pedagogical books[15]) was sometimes indistinguishable from German nationalism, a case in point being the way in which he chose to announce his twelve-note technique in 1923: 'Today I have discovered something which will ensure the superiority of German music for the next hundred years'. It is one of the greater ironies of music history that Schoenberg, who was forced to leave Germany because he was not considered to be sufficiently German, was himself a strong German nationalist. This attitude found great sympathy in the young Webern, whose similar feelings we have already observed, though only in passing. In his description of the Dürer self-portrait that so moved him, he does not see the face as the wonderful image of man, but rather as the wonderful image of *German* man, and Hans Sachs, whose character he finds intensely engaging, he describes as 'this good *German* man'. In a similar vein he reports from Salzburg on the fact that this city contains so many monuments of *German* culture. Later, at the beginning of the First World War, he wrote in a letter to Schoenberg, 'An unshakeable faith in the German spirit, which indeed has created, almost exclusively, the culture of mankind, is awakened in me'.

Another attitude that was already well established in Webern but that must surely have been reinforced by his lifelong intimacy with Schoenberg was a kind of selective misanthropy. In Webern's case, in 1905, this could be explained in large part as a manifestation of the sort of emotional excesses that frequently accompany youth and thus as something that would fade in time – as in Webern's case it did, eventually, though it never disappeared. But with the example of Schoenberg constantly before him – a man who for most of his life seemed to thrive on bad feeling and bitterness – the inclination towards anger and intolerance did not pale so long as the two men were in close contact. Both written and anecdotal examples of Schoenberg's spleen and exaggerated sarcasm are legendary, and too numerous to list. As for Webern, we have seen several instances already and will see many more in the pages to come. A single example from this period will serve as representative here. Following the first performance of Schoenberg's second quartet, which was received with the usual hostility, Webern wrote him, on 27 December 1908:

> Nothing is now more important than showing those swine that we do not allow ourselves to be intimidated. . . . One cannot conceive of the idiocy of men, it is really beyond measure. (HM: 105)

This was the way in which Webern would approach the world for some years to come.

3   1908–14   Instability makes itself known

When men begin to earn a living and become involved with external things, they become empty.

> Webern, in a letter to Schoenberg, 24 December 1910

Having finished university and reached what is usually considered to be the age of maturity, Webern's indecisiveness and instability began to be apparent. He could not tear himself away from Schoenberg and Vienna in 1906, continuing to live on in his father's house and study composition privately for two more years. In the summer of 1908 he began his first job; in the next five years he took up and resigned five positions, in most cases bolting after only a few weeks; made unsuccessful applications for at least eleven others; refused to consider or failed to act on five more; and turned one down outright when it was offered to him. His ditherings in connection with the theatre in Prague are a story in themselves. No diaries survive from these years, but there is copious correspondence, particularly with Berg and Schoenberg.

The pattern of Webern's life during this period was determined almost entirely by his obsessive devotion to Schoenberg and his desire to be near him. This adoration led him to act in such an irresponsible way that even Schoenberg was often exasperated. Although he ceased to be Schoenberg's regular pupil in 1908 his dependence on his former teacher's proximity and pleasure seems to have increased in the decade following, rather than waning, as might be expected. On 19 August 1911 he wrote to Schoenberg, 'I believe that the disciples of Jesus Christ could not have felt more deeply for their Lord than we for you.' Eight days later, 'Whatever I am, everything, everything is through you; I live only through you.' And on 10 June 1914: 'You are set up in my heart as my highest ideal whom I love more and more, to whom I am more and more devoted.'

At the beginning of July 1908 Webern took up his first job, as coach, chorus master and assistant conductor at the summer theatre at Bad Ischl near Salzburg, a fashionable spa frequented by the Emperor Franz Joseph. One of his duties was to be second conductor of the Kurorchester, which provided daily afternoon concerts for the guests, though he seems never to have conducted one of these, since the first conductor did this himself. In a letter written to his cousin on 17 July he refers to his 'stay in this hell' and complains bitterly about how much work he has to do and the fact that he has no time to compose, about the quality of the theatre and about life in general. He says the things he has to do are dreadful, and that mankind would greatly benefit from the destruction of all operettas, farces and folk plays. He had been in the job for two weeks at this time. He was back in Vienna in the autumn of that year, preparing for his first appearance as a conductor there: on 4 November he conducted his Op. 1 Passacaglia in its first performance in the large hall of the Musikverein.

About this time Webern's father was forced by failing health to resign his ministry position, and he decided to give up his Vienna residence as well and retire to the Preglhof. Thus Webern no longer had a home in Vienna. He had to find a job. At the beginning of December he travelled to Berlin to examine the prospects there, but in a letter to Schoenberg dated 8 December he writes that there is nothing: 'Here even well-known conductors are walking around without jobs.'

He was back in Vienna by 21 December for the first performance of Schoenberg's Second String Quartet, and then retired to the Preglhof for Christmas. A letter to Schoenberg from there hints at some connection with the Volksoper, but there is no record of what it was, or even whether it materialised. The next job mentioned was at Innsbruck. This must have been a last-minute replacement, since Webern seems not to have known about it just a few days before he took it up. There is no mention of the engagement in a letter to Schoenberg dated 10 July 1909; but on 25 July Webern wrote to him from Innsbruck, already filled with loathing and desperation. The letter is even more hysterical than the one to Ernst Diez from Bad Ischl.

> God, dear Herr Schoenberg, it is not possible that I should remain here. . . . I will run away from here. My God, it is terrible. I am at my wits' end. . . . It would be a sin against the Holy Ghost if I remain here. It is dreadful! And anyway, what have I to do with such a theatre? O my God, do I have to perform all this filth? It cannot be. What will become of me? If I think of my ideals – or whatever they are called – I would have to perish! I would like to flee – I know not where. . . . I cannot endure this. Please, Herr Schoenberg, send me a few lines . . . I am sure to die here. I am being murdered here.

In this letter there is a hint of something besides moral indignation – a sign that the reasons for his outrage are not to do altogether with his loathing for the tasteless repertoire he is asked to perform. In the middle of the letter he says, 'Just think: a young good-for-nothing, whom I know from Vienna, my "superior"! From him I have to take orders.' This casts a slightly different light on his displeasure and foreshadows similar complaints about future jobs. We can even perhaps reread the letter from Bad Ischl in a new light: the remark on that occasion that he had not been allowed to conduct yet because the first conductor – 'first' in quotation marks – 'takes care of that' may also have been an expression, though a less obvious one, of irritation at not being given the treatment he felt he deserved.

On 28 July, just three days after the cry of anguish and desperation from Innsbruck, Webern wrote to Schoenberg from the Preglhof – obviously he had decamped – without so much as a mention of Innsbruck or the scandal that his rapid departure must have caused. This letter is another lament, but now about a position at Mannheim that has disappeared. 'The director at Mannheim has been discharged and with him all his staff, myself included. So I am again without a position. Now the mess can begin all over again.' This is the first mention of this abortive position.

According to Moldenhauer (HM: 107), there were several job possibilities in the next few months. Webern was made aware of positions open in Troppau, Marburg an der Drau and Koblenz. Apparently he did not make an application for any of them. When Schoenberg heard of the opening at Koblenz, which had been brought to his and Webern's attention by Jalowetz, he sent Webern a telegram, rebuking him for his indifference in the matter of becoming established professionally. Webern responded with a seven-page letter in which he tried to justify his inaction and to regain his position in Schoenberg's good graces. He probably returned to Vienna in September – this was his stated intention in the letter to Schoenberg – and he worked at the Volksoper in the 1909–10 season, likely as an assistant coach. It seems clear from a letter from his father that he was not paid for this work. His father paid his living expenses in Vienna, and in a letter dated 2 January 1910 he expresses concern for his son's well-being:

> For you, dear Toni, I wish more than anything else that your accommodations might be as you wish, and that you also might be given an appropriate position. I beg you however to be mindful always of your health, i.e. to eat and dress properly and not to wear yourself out completely! If the director is so mean and does not pay you, then you should at least lighten your duties somewhat. I should tell him, for example, that you cannot attend the performance *every* evening, since you are obliged to earn your living in some other way and this requires at least three evenings a week. The other coaches, who are being paid for it, should do theatre duty; you are doing enough, with daytime rehearsals!

Webern had spent Christmas and New Year's Day in Vienna, presumably unable to leave Schoenberg and his unpaid but apparently endless tasks at the Volksoper to spend the holidays with his family at the Preglhof. His father regrets his absence but expresses his relief that he has spent Christmas day with his mother's family in Vienna rather than all alone. He then refers to the conductor's position at the Volksoper in Berlin, which Webern must have been hoping for. (Nothing ever came of this; it would seem a rather grand position for him to have been hoping for at this stage, particularly in light of his recent desertions, but the lack of a sense of reality appears to have contributed to all of his difficulties relative to employment.)

The next word from Webern is a letter to Schoenberg dated 10 April, in which he writes cryptically: 'I have much to tell you. For me each day is more terrible than the one before' (HM: 111). No one seems to know what Webern was referring to, but the remark is characteristic. One month later he was writing from Bad Teplitz in northern Bohemia, where he had taken up another position as second conductor of a theatre orchestra. Already, on 13 May, he is complaining, about the job ('It is all so terrible') and about being away from home. Communications dated 19 and 25 May show his spirits much improved; in the first of these he says he has made his conducting début and received sympathetic treatment for it in the newspaper. He describes the performers as 'very nice' and agreeable to all his wishes. He ends that he is 'definitely on top of things here' (HM: 111).

Nevertheless, only one month later, on 14 June, he has left Teplitz in a fit of pique and writes to Schoenberg to explain the affair. A guest singer from Berlin had complained that he received no cues from Webern on his first appearance and that if he was to sing the second role for which he had been hired he would require a full orchestral rehearsal. As time did not allow this the director assigned the second operetta to another conductor. Webern's rage that the guest's opinion was given priority over the previous arrangements made with him caused him to 'walk out of the room without further discussion' (shades of the visit to Pfitzner six years before). He goes on to describe his conducting of the first operetta – the source of the complaint – as 'entirely faultless' on his part and reports that (1) the newspaper review 'singled [him] out again for special notice', (2) he has been told 'from two quarters' that the orchestra spoke very well of him, and (3) the singers were enthusiastic about him, all preferring him to the other conductor. The whole incident he summarises as 'totally without justification' and 'abominable!' (HM: 112).

At this point Webern repaired back to the Preglhof for the remainder of the summer, loudly proclaiming his happiness and relief at now having time to compose. The problem of having no job and no income was not about to go away with the retreat to Carinthia, however, and in the same letter he unabashedly asks Schoenberg for help in securing the post of chorus master at the court in Mannheim, where Schoenberg had connections (and where Webern appears to have been promised some kind of position the year before). Nothing seems to have come of this, and in the middle of September Webern was suddenly offered a position as assistant conductor at the theatre in Danzig (Gdansk), where his friend Jalowetz was second conductor. The new job began immediately; on 24 September he was writing to Schoenberg from his new post, describing Danzig as 'a beautiful big city, teeming with life'. The tone of a letter of 8 October is optimistic:

> It is something quite different here: a complete orchestra, with the strings well-staffed for operetta performances. . . . The musicians are very willing. . . . The operetta is staffed almost entirely with personnel from the opera. This, too, is quite good. The director is wholly delighted with Jalowetz and me. . . . Thank God that I am at last on the right track. (HM: 136)

Nevertheless, true to pattern, he wrote to Berg five days later that he was 'often completely despairing, completely so', and one month later, on 13 November, he wrote to Schoenberg: 'The orchestra here is very unreliable and the public on the whole dreadful. . . . The population here is repugnant to me to the highest degree' (HM: 137). To Berg again, on 20 November, he complained of being 'in this strange city that I hate so much', said that he found his position 'barely endurable' and that he felt 'only half alive'. Things did not bode well for Danzig. He had probably already decided to leave by this time, but Wilhelmine, who had been sent to Paris to study French at the end of the summer, was expecting their child, and he must have realised that he could no longer simply give up employment without any thought for the future. Instead he gave notice, effective in the spring, and began looking for another job. According to Moldenhauer (HM: 142) he actually entered into negotiations with Plauen for the post of second conductor and applied as well for the first conductorship at Klagenfurt, his childhood home, but neither of these positions came to him. To Berg he wrote, on 7 February, 'O God, how often I would like to get out of my skin.'

Webern and Wilhelmine were married in Danzig on 22 February 1911, with Heinrich and Johanna Jalowetz acting as witnesses. The marriage had been the cause of great displeasure on the part of both sets of parents, both because the two were first cousins and because of Wilhelmine's precipitate pregnancy. (Webern wrote to Schoenberg on 17 January 1911 that he was 'not permitted to come home [for Christmas] because of the premarital child'.) Wilhelmine gave birth to a daughter, Amalie, in Berlin on 9 April, and Webern went there a few days later, having finished at Danzig. He then travelled to Vienna, where he, Berg and Horwitz had subsidised a concert of their own compositions for 24 April. He was back in Berlin by 1 May, when he wrote to Schoenberg, reporting that he and Horwitz were making daily rounds to agents and he had filed applications for positions at Braunschweig, Zittau, Lucerne, Aachen and Münster.

On 18 May Gustav Mahler died in Vienna, and Webern returned there once again to attend his funeral, at which he and the rest of the Schoenberg circle occupied a place of honour. After returning to Berlin Webern wrote to Schoenberg, on 24 May: 'Gustav Mahler and you: there I see my course quite distinctly. I will not deviate. God's blessing on you.' In June Webern left Berlin for the third time in two months, this time with Wilhelmine and the child, and went to the Preglhof, where they had been invited by Webern's father to spend the summer. From here two more openings were considered, in Hamburg and Graz. The position at Graz was in fact offered to him, but the conditions did not please him and he turned it down. Relying on the good faith of Schoenberg and Zemlinsky, who was by this time director of the prestigious Deutsches Landestheater in Prague, Webern had also spent the entire summer pleading for work there. Near the end of a letter to Schoenberg dated 9 September Zemlinsky writes:

> I am writing now to Webern to ask whether he wants to come here, as a volunteer for the moment, possibly with occasional pay, but in any case with the possibility of a real engagement later. I am curious as to what his answer will be. (Zem: 63)

Webern went to Prague for the first time on 13 September 1911. This was the beginning of an incredible series of tergiversations in connection with this city. On 18 September he wrote to Schoenberg, saying that he was back in Vienna, but anxiously assuring him that this was not as the result of improper deportment on his part in Prague. He says that the job offered in Prague was a good one and would have been well paid but that he couldn't face a life in the theatre. Then he comes to what was probably the real reason for his having turned down the job: 'Above everything: I would like to be with you. I picture the winter thus: I will be in whichever city you are in and will mainly make reductions of your works. Naturally, I would like to compose as much as possible' (HM: 149). That a young man of twenty-eight who was on the threshold of his own career as a composer should find more appealing than any other possibility that of spending the winter making reductions of someone else's music gives some idea of the degree to which Schoenberg's pupils were besotted with him.

It was Webern's misfortune that in 1911 the two essentials for his happiness – Schoenberg and Vienna – could not be enjoyed at the same time. In July the Schoenbergs had moved to Berlin. So on 6 October Webern went back to Berlin, where he stayed with the Schoenbergs for a few days until he found an apartment nearby. Here he was joined by Wilhelmine and Amalie. In letters to Berg and Paul Königer, another Schoenberg pupil who had gone to Berg when Schoenberg left Vienna and who later married Wilhelmine's sister, he

4   Anton von Webern, 1912.

writes both of his great joy at being with Schoenberg again and of his constant longing for Vienna. Living off the income from a few pupils and from Wilhelmine's dowry (which must have been generous, since the couple purchased a piano upon moving to Berlin), Webern again became aware, however, during the course of the winter of the need for regular employment. Again he turned to Prague. In a letter dated simply January 1912 Zemlinsky tells Schoenberg that Webern has written to him and that he intends to answer, but that what Webern wants is simply not possible at the moment (Zem: 74). Still persisting in his petition Webern offered to play the celesta part in a performance of Mahler's Eighth Symphony conducted by Zemlinsky in Prague in late March, doubtless wishing to keep lines of communication with

Zemlinsky open. Nevertheless, immediately following this performance he wrote to Berg from Prague announcing a surprise move: he had accepted a theatre position in Stettin (Szczecin) from late June. Here he would be working with Jalowetz once again.

Before going to the new job in Stettin the Weberns spent several weeks in Austria. For the first time they did not go to the Preglhof: Webern's father had sold the estate earlier in the year and set up a household in Klagenfurt which included his two daughters and the husband and children of the elder. The Weberns spent three weeks there before going on to Vienna for a time. They arrived in Stettin on 21 June (via Berlin for one last visit with the Schoenbergs), the day before Webern was scheduled to take up his new activities.

The by now predictable stream of complaining letters begins after only a few days. At first they are filled with the old familiar woes: Webern is overworked; the music is 'nauseating', 'abominable'; he is forced to live among 'the scum of men'; he is being mistreated by those above him in the hierarchy. 'The director is a cretin beyond compare. A man with no understanding at all. A fop. His main concern seems to be that the conductors should always be well shaven' (HM: 162). This director also made the considerable mistake of addressing Webern as 'little man'; Webern reported this to Schoenberg, adding, 'To be sure, he is six times bigger than I, but certainly innumerable times more stupid' (17 July). Yet he can write in all seriousness to Schoenberg less than two weeks later (on 31 July): 'Fundamentally, I think badly of no one, wish well to absolutely everyone. Why do they treat me so rudely? . . . This has never happened to me before' (HM: 164). And, just as incredibly (remembering the letters written from Danzig two years earlier), on 16 November, about the orchestra: 'It is really quite miserable. Its incompetence is beyond compare. . . . The performance in Danzig was much nicer and therefore, . . . I was then in the right mood. Here not at all' (HM: 165). Webern's letters to Schoenberg, Berg and others are very frequent (indeed, one wonders where he found the time to write letters nearly every day – and whether he might not have felt himself less overworked had he spent less time reporting every detail of his life to his friends), and they carry on in this vein from practically the beginning of his tenure in Stettin. To Berg, on 19 July:

> As a non-participant, I would flee a theatre such as the one where I am at present as if it were a place infested with the plague, and now I myself must help to stir the sauce. Often I am ashamed, I appear to myself like a criminal even collaborating in this hell-hole of mankind. I can hardly await my deliverance from this morass. (HM: 162)

Most of the complaints are old ones, well worn from use in previous venues, but one new source of distress surfaces now, as well. Webern complains bitterly about his nerves and his poor health. The first such complaint comes as early as 3 July, when he writes to Schoenberg that he feels 'worse than ever' and that he gets into such a state of exhaustion (for 'exhaustion' perhaps one should read 'choler') that he cannot move. His feet ache so that he can hardly walk. By the beginning of October he is complaining that not only his feet but his whole body is affected: 'Head, arms, and legs ache terribly. And now insomnia has gripped me again. I cannot lie down' (HM: 166). He seems to be suffering a mental collapse as well. On 12 September he claims, 'I am often in complete despair about myself, about my talent, about my character, about everything.' Probably under the influence of Strindberg, with whose writing he was much taken at the moment, he began to see occurrences in the theatre as omens, and his torment in Stettin as a punishment.

Alarmed, both his father and Schoenberg, not for the first time, counselled him urgently not to put yet another job at risk. After the sale of the family estate (in which the elder Webern had originally hoped to see his son safely ensconced and thus assured of a comfortable life) Webern's father had settled 50,000 kronen (about £2,080 in 1912, or the equivalent of nearly £65,000 in 1997) on each of his three children. This was perhaps in Webern's case an unwise thing to do, as it gave him a kind of temporary security that made it easier for him to ignore the obvious necessity for some kind of continuing livelihood. Wilhelmine was now expecting a second child as well.

By November Webern had decided to leave Stettin at the earliest possible opportunity. At his father's urging he registered with an agent in Berlin and in the following weeks filed applications for positions in Düsseldorf, Dortmund and Bochum. An opening in Riga, for an operetta conductor, was turned down without consideration. On 12 December something happened that set a pattern that was to be repeated often in the course of Webern's future life as a conductor: he was unable to conduct an evening performance. He reports on this to Schoenberg the following day:

> Already I lie sick in bed again. My nerve attacks become more and more acute. For several nights by now I have had almost no sleep; the night before last I even had a fever. As a result, I am so exhausted that yesterday towards evening I went to bed instead of conducting *Waffenschmied*. What ill luck I have! (HM: 167)

On 17 January 1913 Webern requested sick leave from Stettin, and one week later he entered Dr Vecsey's sanatorium at Semmering, a mountain resort situated about halfway between Vienna and Graz. Wilhelmine, whose second child was due in February, stayed in Stettin. Within a month Webern had decided not to return there at all but to go directly to Vienna upon his release from the sanatorium. It is not clear on what date he officially asked for a conversion of his sick leave to a resignation. In the meantime, however, he had been in contact with Zemlinsky in Prague yet again. As early as 7 March Zemlinsky writes to Schoenberg, 'You probably know already that Webern has been engaged here for next season? I am very pleased about this. I hope he is in good health' (Zem: 88).

On 9 March Webern returned to Vienna, to be joined there by his family a week later. (A second daughter, Maria, had been born on 17 February.) His re-entry into the life of Vienna was not a peaceful one. He was involved immediately in preparations for what was to become a notorious concert on 31 March. The programme, conducted entirely by Schoenberg, consisted of Webern's Op. 6 orchestral pieces, Zemlinsky's Maeterlinck songs with orchestra, Schoenberg's First Chamber Symphony, two of Berg's *Altenberg Lieder* and Mahler's *Kindertotenlieder*. The concert resulted in one of the two biggest scandals in the history of music, the other being the first performance of Stravinsky's *Rite of Spring* in Paris two months later. Repercussions continued in the newspapers and the law courts for months;[1] a few days later Berg wrote to Webern that he would like 'to fly far away', which is precisely what Webern had done. Following the concert and its disagreeable aftermath Webern fled the city, taking his family to Portorose, a resort town on the Adriatic near Trieste. Their hope of staying there for some time in the sun was dashed by constant bad weather, however, and on 23 April they joined Webern's father's household in Klagenfurt. They had no permanent home at this time, as Webern was between the jobs at Stettin and Prague.

The household at Klagenfurt was too active and noisy for Webern, who was not able to compose in such surroundings, so very soon he and his family moved on to stay with Wilhelmine's aunt and her family in Mürzzuschlag. Here Webern was able to rent an attic room in a house high up the mountain as a studio in which to be alone and work. From Mürzzuschlag he also had easy access to the alpine walks that were always such an essential part of his life. The family stayed here for two months. On 6 June he wrote to Zemlinsky from Mürzzuschlag:

> You ask me whether I want to come to Prague for the beginning of the season. When is it exactly? My contract runs from 1 September. I should arrive at the latest four days before. It was my intention to come already in the middle of August. And I am happy to come even earlier. (Zem: 282)

He goes on to register delight at having been offered a new stage production as well as the opportunity to coach and rehearse *Parsifal*.

The idyll in Mürzzuschlag was interrupted by the tragic and sudden death of Webern's older sister Maria's twelve-year-old son, Theo Clementschitsch, of a ruptured appendix while on holiday with his parents in Italy. Webern went to Klagenfurt for the funeral and to be with the family for a week in July, then returned to Mürzzuschlag, as he reported to Schoenberg, 'completely exhausted'. On 25 July he took his family to Vienna, and by 28 July he was in Prague. On this date he wrote to Schoenberg that he had found a flat, and he immediately returned to Vienna and made arrangements for the removal of their household belongings to Prague. Notwithstanding the contract mentioned in the letter above, he was to begin the new job on 4 August.

On 31 July Webern wrote to Schoenberg once again. He had now decided that he was too ill to take the job in Prague. From letters written by Zemlinsky to Schoenberg and Webern respectively on 6 and 7 August it is clear that, though Webern had told Schoenberg of his decision several days earlier, he had not yet told Zemlinsky, who heard the news only from Schoenberg and Wilhelmine. In his letter to Webern Zemlinsky demonstrates truly admirable and almost unbelievable patience with the young man who had taken flight without a word of warning five days before the opening of the new season (and not for the first time). He describes the turmoil that Webern's unexpected departure has caused the theatre, but first of all he tells Webern that he has hired a *temporary substitute* (Zemlinsky's emphasis) to fulfil Webern's duties in the coming season, and he expresses sorrow and disappointment, and a genuine concern for Webern's health. He advises Webern not to 'play around' with his nerves, but to take the year off and regain his strength. Finally, he expresses the hope that when Webern is completely recovered he may wish to return to Prague to take up the position there (Zem: 282–3).

Ethics aside, Webern was now in a very unenviable position. In a letter to Zemlinsky dated 13 August Schoenberg told his friend that he found it extremely difficult to advise Webern of a solution to his difficulties. Webern had had to pay three months' rent on the flat he rented in Prague; in addition, he had moved all his furniture there, and to move it back was going to be a further expense. Schoenberg had advised him that perhaps the best solution would be to take a year's lease and leave his household belongings in Prague, since if his health improved he could take up the position there in a year's time. However there was always the possibility that his health might not improve sufficiently (Zem: 101).

Webern had of course returned to Vienna. This time Schoenberg advised him to seek medical advice and actually try to get to the root of his problems. Thorough examination by a nerve specialist resulted in his being told that there was no sign of any physical disorder, and that perhaps the best plan of action was to see a psychoanalyst.

All this happened in the space of a few days: on 6 August – the date of Zemlinsky's letter to Schoenberg and the day *before* Zemlinsky had penned his letter to Webern acknowledging his absence and releasing him from his contract – Webern was writing to Schoenberg already about his second session with Dr Alfred Adler, the psychologist he had decided – with many reservations at first – to entrust with his treatment. He saw Dr Adler every day, and his reports to Schoenberg about the treatment are extensive. Dr Adler had suggested three months as an appropriate period of time; on 30 October Webern declared himself cured.

Wilhelmine and the children had stayed in Mürzzuschlag when Webern went to Prague. Shortly after his return the family moved in with Wilhelmine's parents in Vienna. At the end of August they took a small flat – two rooms, kitchen and bath – in Hietzing, the thirteenth district of Vienna, west of the centre of the city. Webern now began once again to think about future employment. Steuermann informed him of an opening in Aachen, but he failed to do anything about it, probably out of pique at the response of the theatre there to his application of two years earlier. It is unclear what was in his mind at this time. He had a standing offer from Prague, a theatre in which he had on two previous occasions been promised interesting work and a decent salary, yet he approached Jalowetz about returning to Stettin, a theatre which he had reviled in the most contemptuous terms for the duration of his tenure there and from which he had eventually fled in desperation. There is no record of his having informed Zemlinsky that it was after all not his intention to return to Prague when he was able.

On 23 April 1914 he signed a contract with the theatre in Stettin for the post of second conductor, commencing in June. He persuaded the theatre director to allow him to provide a stand-in until 20 August. With the help of Jalowetz an apartment was rented in Stettin, and at the end of June the flat in Hietzing was vacated, the household effects were once again bundled into a removals van, and the family went to the household in Klagenfurt for a holiday before taking up the new job. On 23 July Austria-Hungary delivered an ultimatum to Serbia; on 28 July war was declared and the theatre at Stettin was closed.

In addition to his large-scale peregrinations during these years Webern made frequent excursions of several days' or weeks' duration to various centres to attend important performances, usually of works by Schoenberg or Mahler. During the years when the members of the Schoenberg circle were dispersed these events often represented reunions. These trips, which must have sorely stretched Webern's meagre resources during this period of financial uncertainty, were clearly of the utmost importance to him, taking precedence over all other considerations. He had not the slightest misgivings, for example, about swanning off just a few days after taking up a new theatre position, leaving someone else to fill in for him.

Webern's first such trip was in 1910, when he travelled alone to Munich from Vienna to see Mahler conduct the première of his Eighth Symphony on 12 September. This was a particularly important visit for Webern, who held Mahler in the greatest esteem: it was the last time the two men were to speak together, and Mahler, who seems also to have been fond of Webern, gave him an ink sketch of his song 'Lob des hohen Verstandes', something that Webern was to treasure all his life. Some six weeks later, on 31 October, when Webern had just taken up his new post at Danzig, Schoenberg's *Pelleas und Melisande* was performed in Berlin with Schoenberg present, and Webern made the long journey from Danzig to Berlin for the occasion.

On 20 November 1911 Bruno Walter conducted the first performance of Mahler's *Lied von der Erde* in Munich. Webern, who was by now living in Berlin, went several days early and took in several rehearsals as well as the performance. He was met later by Berg and Paul Königer, who travelled from Vienna. Webern was ecstatic about the work. To Königer, on 23 November, he wrote: '*Das Lied von der Erde* is the most marvellous creation that exists. . . . It can not be described in words. What power exerts itself here!' To Berg he wrote that he would like to have breathed his last after hearing the contrabassoon passage at 'Aus tiefstem Schauen lauscht' ich auf'. In fact, the work was so wonderful that he wondered whether they should be entitled to hear it at all. (This echoes his response to Bayreuth in 1902.) Later the same winter Webern accompanied Schoenberg to Prague for another performance of *Pelleas und Melisande*, on 29 February 1912. They went a week ahead, and again Webern attended rehearsals. At first he stayed with Horwitz, later moving to a hotel. (Horwitz had assumed the position in Prague that Webern had turned down some months earlier.) Later Berg, Königer, Karl Linke (another Schoenberg pupil) and Polnauer also came, from Vienna, as well as Webern's and Königer's wives.

Webern made two more big trips from Berlin, both in March of 1912 and both to attend performances of Mahler's Eighth Symphony. Near the beginning of the month he travelled to Vienna for two performances of the work. On this occasion he stayed in Vienna for more than two weeks. Near the end of the month he and Schoenberg travelled to Prague for rehearsals and two more performances of the same work. It was on this occasion that Webern played the celesta part.

In late June 1912, about a week after taking up his new post at Stettin, Webern travelled to Vienna for two concerts that he and Berg had arranged as a 'counter-festival' to the official Vienna Music Festival Week. Webern's Four Pieces for Violin and Piano, Op. 7, were presented in the second of these. On this occasion he was given leave from his new job to attend, even though he was scheduled to conduct in Stettin on 30 June. Unfortunately, as he reported to Schoenberg on 3 July, the composer Franz Schreker's wife got the giggles during his pieces. On 7 July he wrote to Schoenberg from Stettin concerning the second concert: 'Your quartet [No. 2] touched my father deeply. He also liked Berg's sonata. My pieces are too "nervous" for him. "It is always all over before it starts", he says' (HM: 161). (Schoenberg, living in Berlin at this time, had not been present at either concert.) In the autumn of the same year Webern travelled to Berlin for the first performance of *Pierrot Lunaire*, conducted by Schoenberg there on 16 October.

A few months later, after his retreat from Stettin to Semmering, Webern travelled to Vienna to attend the première of Schoenberg's *Gurrelieder* at the Musikverein on 23 February 1913. On this occasion he was given leave from Dr Vecsey's sanatorium to attend the concert, a quite exceptional practice as he was not considered cured. One month later he was back in Vienna, this time having been discharged from Semmering, to take part in the famous *Skandalkonzert* of 31 March.

Two more trips were undertaken the following year, when Webern was living in Vienna. At the end of January 1914 he travelled to Prague with Stein, Berg and Königer to meet Schoenberg, who still lived in Berlin, for a performance of the latter's Six Songs with Orchestra, Op. 8, under Zemlinsky. In a letter from Berg to his wife dated 27 January in Prague, he writes of his friend (who had declared himself cured on 30 October): 'Webern is badly ill. Had a terribly high temperature the last two or three days, and was quite thinking of going back home. Now it's angina, and he can hardly drag himself about' (Berg: 150). In March Webern and Stein accompanied Schoenberg on a two-week concert tour to Leipzig, Amsterdam (for performances of *Gurrelieder* and Schoenberg's Five Pieces for Orchestra, Op. 16) and Berlin.

Webern did of course do other things during these years besides travel and move house. Except for his marriage in 1911 and the birth of his first two children in 1911 and 1913, most of his personal activities were Schoenberg-inspired or -related. It was one of his missions in life to serve Schoenberg in whatever ways he could, often at his own expense and frequently, it would appear, with little appreciation in return. One of the earliest occasions on which he was very energetic in helping his friend was in a cause that some might not find completely

5   Erwin Stein, Arnold Schoenberg and Anton von Webern in Holland, 1914.

laudable: the Gerstl affair in 1908. In the summer of this year Schoenberg's wife Mathilde, the sister of Zemlinsky and the mother of two young children (six and two years of age), left her husband in favour of the painter Richard Gerstl, a close family friend who had been living in the same building as the Schoenbergs for a time and giving both of them painting lessons (though Schoenberg with characteristic modesty later claimed that Gerstl got most of his inter- esting ideas and techniques from him). From all accounts Schoen- berg was both astonished and devastated at his wife's defection. It was Webern who, pursuing her in the middle of the night and argu- ing her moral obligation to her children, succeeded in bringing her back. Gerstl killed himself in the autumn of the same year, and vis- itors to the Schoenberg home in years to come have described

Mathilde as morose, taciturn, withdrawn and silent – 'a frail, sick-looking woman who sat silently in the corner of the couch, always wrapped in a shawl'[2] freezing, while Schoenberg did everything in the house (Smith: 140). While Webern doubtless felt gratified with his part in what he surely saw as a moral victory, others may find his intervention less easy to justify. He interceded on Schoenberg's behalf in another quarter that year as well: in a letter to Schoenberg written on 13 December 1908 from Berlin (where Webern had gone to hunt for a job) he intimates that he has asked his father to have a word with the president of the Vienna Academy about a teaching post there for Schoenberg. A lectureship in composition at the Academy followed in 1910.

Friendship with Schoenberg was a very demanding business; there seems to have been no task too onerous or too burdensome for him to ask of his devotees. It was apparently perfectly clear to him (as indeed it seems to have been to them as well) that his music and his business were of greater importance than theirs and that whatever time or energy – or money – they contributed towards his well-being was well spent. He was almost continually in financial difficulty and much of the time enmeshed in personal or political entanglements as well; his friends were expected to bail him out. As Webern's own financial situation was always precarious, this was often a hardship for him. But he supplied money gratefully, as he did time and energy, which were also sometimes in short supply.

There were many contributing factors to Schoenberg's flight from Vienna in the summer of 1911, but the immediate reason was the continued insults and threats of an apparently deranged neighbour in the apartment house where he lived in Hietzing. (This man's violent behaviour was directed not only at Schoenberg: he was eventually given two weeks' notice and made to leave the apartment house. The neighbour's primary complaint against Schoenberg seems to have been that the indecent behaviour of Schoenberg's nine-year-old daughter was corrupting his two sons, who were five and eleven.) Schoenberg finally left the premises hurriedly and in a state of disarray;

violence was avoided at the moment of departure only by the presence of Josef Polnauer, a burly man who served the Schoenberg circle in a similar way on several occasions. Schoenberg's only source of income – his private teaching – came to an abrupt halt with his flight from Vienna, and Webern and Jalowetz immediately organised an appeal for funds.

This was not the only fund-raising campaign to be organised for Schoenberg's benefit; there were several such in operation at this time and over the next several years, set up at Schoenberg's suggestion and involving appeals to individual wealthy patrons, advertisements in journals and a number of other strategies. In fact Schoenberg seemed to be of the opinion that the world owed him the means for a life style that reflected his superiority. One of the favourite targets of his considerable resentment was 'millionaires': he often goes on bitterly and at great length in his letters, railing against 'rich people' and their inability to comprehend his entitlement to their help. On 31 October 1911 (BSC: 37–8) he complained at length to Berg that the people he had asked to raise money for him – his request had been that 'several rich people' be induced to give him 'an annual salary of at least 6,000 kronen (£250, the equivalent of nearly £8000 in 1997 terms) for several years' – had not done nearly as well as he had expected. He asked Berg what was the matter with the campaign and urged him to work harder at it and produce better results.

> I must state: I have never begged. And have never asked for money because I was starving. [It might be pointed out that some of those who were canvassing on his behalf, and contributing to his income – Webern, for example – were doing very nearly that.] I merely want to lead a calm and modest life, much more modest than that of millionaires, though I accomplish much more! And I want to offer my family that modicum of comfort that millionaires would consider depressing poverty if they had to live like that themselves.

Further:

> I expressly declared what I wanted the money for: in order to live well!

Berg's response to this letter on 3 November, beginning with 'Thank you very much, dear, kind Herr Schoenberg, for your dear, long letter' (BSC: 40–1), is typical of the reaction of Schoenberg's students to his arrogance and ill-temper during these years. (It has to be said that Schoenberg seems to have mellowed into a much more humane individual a few decades later.) Berg immediately renewed his efforts on Schoenberg's behalf, and in addition to the campaign to interest 'millionaires' he and Webern, Jalowetz, Stein and others – all of whom were younger and not yet established and, without campaigns mounted on their own behalf, less well off than Schoenberg – continued to subsidise Schoenberg whenever they could.

Upon fleeing from Vienna, the Schoenbergs at first stayed with Zemlinsky, who was on holiday at the Starnbergersee, but in late September Schoenberg decided to move on to Berlin, without returning to Vienna. His students, Berg and Webern in particular, were left to tie up the loose ends left by his hasty departure. These included packing up the contents of his study and arranging for the shipment of all the household goods to Berlin, as well as paying six months' rent in order to get a clearance of the lease on the apartment. He also asked them to try to find someone to rent it for part of this time. All of this they did, while Schoenberg directed operations, often irritably, by letter from Berlin. In the meantime, with the money they had raised for him, Schoenberg rented an entire floor of a spacious residence with extensive grounds in Zehlendorf, a suburb of Berlin. In both Vienna and Berlin the fund-raising campaign was to continue for some years.

When Webern moved to Berlin in October of 1911 his two expressed desires were to be with Schoenberg and to have time for composition, in that order. In the event the fulfilment of the first of these left no time for the second. In the autumn and winter of 1909 he had made a piano reduction of parts of Schoenberg's still unfinished *Gurrelieder*, for a performance in Vienna on 14 January 1910. Now Schoenberg asked him to perform a similar task with his Op. 16 pieces for orchestra, *Verklärte Nacht* and *Pelleas und Melisande*. It is safe to assume that the preparation of these reductions took most of Webern's time in the winter of 1911–12. Only the reduction of Op. 16 was finished; it was performed in Berlin on 4 February 1912. In addition Webern became preoccupied during this time with the idea of a literary tribute to his teacher.

In a letter dated 19 September 1911 Schoenberg had asked Berg if he would consider writing five to eight pages about him 'right away' for a music periodical. It was to be a 'clear characterisation' of his musical personality: 'origins, development, and present style' (BSC: 13). Gerhard Tischer, editor of the *Rheinische Musik- und Theaterzeitung*, had asked for such an article in the hope of furthering Schoenberg's cause. In this letter Schoenberg says that he is also asking Webern, and that they should decide between themselves who is to do it. In the end the task fell to Webern. In May of 1911, when the friends had been gathered together in Vienna for Mahler's funeral, Schoenberg had suggested that his pupils should assemble a book of testimonials for the purpose of advancing his position as a teacher. Webern had taken this task very seriously and by the autumn was already heavily involved in the project. In the end Berg and Webern edited jointly a literary tribute to Schoenberg, though no editors' names appeared on the book. A specially bound copy was presented to Schoenberg in February of 1912.

Webern produced no music of his own during his winter in Berlin. He had however by the time he went there written all the music that would later bear the opus numbers 1 to 10. Upon leaving Schoenberg's class Webern had returned immediately to composing songs with piano accompaniment. He had set two poems by Richard Dehmel in 1906 and 1907; in 1908 he composed three more. He also turned his attention once again to the poetry of Stefan George, whose poem he had used for the text of *Entflieht auf leichten Kähnen* in 1908. In 1908–9 he set fourteen George poems, ten of which he would later publish as his Opp. 3 and 4. All these were written in Vienna or at the Preglhof. Though his music had been increasingly atonal for some time prior to this, and key signatures had in several instances already been either absent or meaningless, in the George songs he finally abandoned them forever. These songs represent a new direction: they are quite different in many ways from the previous music (indeed, from even the roughly contemporary Dehmel songs) and are the first of the works in Webern's 'aphoristic style'. Although his earliest attempts at composition had produced relatively short pieces, of twenty or thirty bars' length, a few of the songs from his university years had been two or three times this length and several of the instrumental pieces written during his study with Schoenberg were quite extended. The songs of Op. 3 vary in length from ten to sixteen bars, those of Op. 4 are very slightly longer; two of the four that were left over are twenty-two and thirty bars in length – perhaps one reason for their being excluded from the published sets. All ten are studies in near-silence (half of them use a dynamic range extending only from *ppp* to *p*, with *p* used very sparingly; in all ten *ppp* is the level that predominates). Registrally they cover a wide range in a brief time, the piano accompaniment regularly spread over five or six octaves. Although textures are dense and rhythms complex, the remarkable reduction in dynamics and the atonal nature of the chords result in shimmering and quickly changing colours rather than the turgidity that the appearance of the score suggests. This new compression and dissonance were to be essential features of Webern's music from this time onward.

When he was not distracted by conducting in the theatre these were prolific years for Webern. Though the form his reaction took was usually imprudent, his irritation and depression at not having any time to compose during his tenure in his early conducting positions must be viewed sympathetically: when he did have the time, he had something to say. Besides the completion of the George songs, the summer of 1909 at the Preglhof saw the composition of the minute and otherworldly Op. 5 movements for string quartet and the completion of the first draft of the Six Pieces for Large Orchestra, Op. 6, written as a memorial to Webern's mother and dedicated 'to Arnold Schoenberg, my teacher and friend, with the greatest affection'. On the other hand, the two winters when he did not hold conducting jobs – 1909–10, spent in Vienna with Schoenberg after decamping from Innsbruck, and 1911–12, spent in Berlin with Schoenberg after refusing to take up the job at Prague – were just as fruitless as the seasons when he was employed in the theatre. Although Webern certainly would not have seen it in this way, Schoenberg was as voracious of Webern's time as the theatre. In both these years his only creative output was the piano reductions he produced of Schoenberg's music. His own violin pieces, Op. 7, and the two Rilke songs, Op. 8, were written in the summer of 1910, during his summer at the Preglhof. The following summer, 1911, saw the composition of four of the Bagatelles for String Quartet, Op. 9, again at the Preglhof, with the remaining two movements of this work produced also in the summer, two years later when the family was staying at Mürzzuschlag. Two of the orchestral pieces of Op. 10 date from the summer of 1911 as well, the rest being written in Vienna in the autumn of 1913. The final aphoristic work was the Three Little Pieces for Violoncello and Piano, Op. 11, written in Vienna during the spring and summer of 1914. All of these pieces, comprising Webern's published work from 1909–14, continue on the course set by the two sets of George songs. They are increasingly minimalist in nearly every respect; they are fleeting glimpses, whispered suggestions, breaths – with George and Schoenberg – of 'the air of another planet'.

In his introduction to the Op. 9 Bagatelles Schoenberg writes of 'a novel in a single gesture, a joy in a breath'. His brief description is in fact more perspicacious than it might at first appear to be (or, perhaps, than he even intended). While comparison with a novel implies a compression of content, the image of 'a joy' supposes nothing of the kind. Each of these sets of tiny pieces strikes a balance between movements of two sorts: those in which the most extreme registral and dynamic differences have been condensed into a few frenzied gestures in as many bars, and those in which time and activity seem to be suspended for a few seconds. Pieces of the first sort are generally longer than those of the second and written in a quick tempo, with thick textures and impassioned activity, and extremes of register and dynamics (***ppp*** to ***fff***) in close proximity. The second type of piece is usually between eight and fourteen bars in length (several are eight or nine bars, one is only six), contains a minimum of notes (the fourth piece of Op. 10 consists of twenty-eight notes, two of these expressed as a trill), and may also cover a wide registral canvas, but confines its dynamic activity to ***ppp*** and ***pp*** (in the case of Op. 7 no. 3 never rising above ***ppp***). A multiplicity of instrumental effects – harmonics, pizzicato, spiccato, non- vibrato, col legno (bowing or striking the strings with the wood of the bow), *am Griffbrett* (bowing over the fingerboard) and *am Steg* (bowing at the bridge) in the string parts; fluttertongue in the flutes; mutes used liberally in all parts – abounds in the pieces of both types, resulting in an eerie sound world in which timbre frequently predominates over pitch, and silence assumes a place on a par with both. The final aphoristic work – the three Op. 11 pieces, which total thirty-two bars altogether – is also the most extreme. In the third of these pieces, which is entirely ***ppp*** and ***pp***, the cello plays eight notes and the piano a three-note melody and three chords, all in or below the bass clef. Plate 6 is a facsimile of this piece.

The small number of notes in some of these pieces is probably their most striking feature when compared to the music of other composers of the time, and can be seen as a direct expression of the crisis that the Viennese triumvirate created for themselves in abandoning tonality. Webern said later of his experience when composing the Op. 9 Bagatelles: 'I had the feeling that when all twelve notes had gone by the piece was finished. ... In my sketchbook I wrote out the chromatic scale and crossed off the individual notes.' While none of the atonal aphorisms attempts serial composition, the constant circulation of the twelve notes is a significant feature of all of them. Other significant characteristics are the preponderance of semitones and their permutations (sevenths, ninths and so on); a lack of rhythmic pulse and metric definition; single chords and short melodic figures isolated by silence on either side; continual changes of timbre and the juxtaposition of extremes (of register, timbre, dynamics). While long repeated-note figures and measured tremolos in which two notes

6 Partitur of the third of the Op. 11 pieces for cello and piano, 1914.

alternate are surprisingly frequent, repetition of longer figures is abjured. This includes imitation, sequence, variation and even motivic development. Short melodic figures look like motives but are not treated as such.

There were several other projects during these years, not all of them aphoristic in nature. In the letter to Ernst Diez written from Bad Ischl on 17 July 1908 Webern mentions two opera projects. One is in the future: he says, obviously in answer to a recent letter from his cousin, 'I am very happy that you would like to write an opera libretto for me.' This will be his second opera, he goes on to say. The first, which is already underway, is a setting of Maeterlinck's *Alladine and Palomides*, a project about which he says 'Schoenberg is very happy'. He then sets down certain restrictions for the forthcoming libretto:

> I make the following conditions, however: *no processions, no battles, nothing that in any way requires 'illustration'.* I need only a couple of characters. But not a theatre piece! Maeterlinck writes more or less in this vein. But I want it even more so. Completely other than what is now called theatre. The opposite.

> Do you understand me? If your libretto is like this, then it will be right for me. Everything else disgusts me to the highest degree.

Only the beginning of a sketch for *Alladine and Palomides* survives; there is no sign of the libretto by Ernst Diez.

Two years later Webern wrote to Schoenberg of another opera project. On 6 July 1910: 'I am writing something for the theatre. It is a Maeterlinck subject. Once I am further along with it, I will write to you what it is.' And, ten days later, 'I have begun *The Seven Princesses*. Work proceeds well.' This opera, which was never completed, is mentioned on several occasions. As late as July 1912 Webern referred in a letter to Berg to the 'several scenes' of this work that he had completed. Nothing of it survives.

It is difficult to imagine an opera by Webern, though he was once such an avid lover of opera. Perhaps it is not surprising that his only brushes with composing in the medium were connected with Maeterlinck. Although Schoenberg had used Maeterlinck's *Pelléas et Mélisande* as the silent text for one of his great early tone poems, Maeterlinck's aesthetic seems to be much more akin to Webern's than to Schoenberg's. (Indeed, in Schoenberg's hands *Pelleas* is transformed into a German Romantic drama.) When Webern was in Berlin in 1908 one of the many works he saw there was Debussy's much more faithful *Pelléas*. He was greatly impressed. On 6 December he wrote to

Schoenberg, 'Oh God, I cannot express how beautiful it was!' And two days later:

> ... very fine, often very strange, in places wonderfully beautiful. ...
> The ending is one of the loveliest that exists. ... Maeterlinck's drama
> also possesses such unheard-of beauty—such atmosphere, such
> tenderness, then again so much passion. ... It is marvellous! (HM:
> 104)

Thus, it seems, he had found his playwright.

Webern worked on several projects – in addition to the movements written to complete Opp. 9 and 10 – during the season that he spent in Vienna during and after his treatment by Dr Adler. The strangest of these was a stage play, *Tot*, in six tableaux, which was inspired by the death of his nephew the previous summer and written while he was actually seeing Adler. It is heavily indebted to Emanuel Swedenborg, whose work is in fact extensively quoted at one point. When shown the piece, Schoenberg questioned whether the inclusion of such a long passage from someone else's work did not constitute plagiarism. Though Webern sent the work to Schoenberg to read, he made no further use of it. The complete play survives but has never been published. Completed musical works written during this season include five orchestra pieces and three orchestral songs, all settings of poems written by Webern in the summer of 1913: 'Schmerz, immer blick nach oben', 'O sanftes Glühn der Berge' and 'Leise Düfte'. These works were not given opus numbers or published by Webern; they were published by Moldenhauer in 1968 and 1971. Webern also worked long and hard during this time on a cello sonata, in which he attempted to extend his new atonal idiom to longer forms. He had finished one movement of this by 9 May 1914, but in that summer he finally admitted defeat and produced instead the cello pieces of Op. 11, his most extreme aphorisms. Several brief orchestral fragments from the winter of 1913–14 also survive in sketch form only, most only two to four bars in length.

For Webern the period between 1908, when his lessons with Schoenberg ended, and 1914, when his world was suddenly rent by the Great War, was a time of tough lessons in reality incompletely learned. It was a period of transition, a short period of freedom separating two quite different disciplines, the regularity of formal lessons in composition and the regimented life of the military. This is reflected in the music that dates from these years, music that spans the gap between the tonal forms of Webern's youth and the text-determined structures of the period after 1914, through a no-man's-land of aphoristic and unstructured miniatures. These years produced the music for which Webern will probably always be best known, and which was most uniquely his. And this music, with its restless, unpredictable but continual movement from one place to another, one instrument to another, one dynamic and range to another – only a brief moment spent in each place before taking a new direction – seems to describe a remarkably accurate parallel to the composer's life during these years.

4   1914–21   Vacillations continue

Oh, everything will end well.

Webern, 8 September 1914

We have already had occasion to observe Webern's fervent German nationalism. When Austria-Hungary declared war on Serbia on 28 July 1914, with most of the other countries of Europe joining in the fray only days later, he was seized immediately by the desire to join up and fight for the moral right, an action that his family and friends succeeded in delaying only until February of the following year. He had never a moment's doubt about where the right lay.

> Day and night the wish haunts me: to be able to fight for this great, sublime cause. Do you not agree that this war really has no political motivations? It is the struggle of the angels with the devils. For everything that has revealed itself about the enemy nations during the course of these weeks really demonstrates only one thing: that they are liars and swindlers. . . .—what nauseating filth! By contrast, the open, honourable position of our nations. . . . Catholic France! They have raged against Germans and Austrians like cannibals. . . . And the most ridiculous of all – these Englishmen! (HM: 210)

So he wrote to Schoenberg on 8 September 1914. Berg, who seems always to have been more perceptive and realistic than Webern, took a very different view of the war. On New Year's Eve of 1914 he wrote to his wife:

[The war] frightens me more than ever, now I've realized it is going to last for ages longer.

I couldn't imagine that its task would be fulfilled all that quickly: the task of making the world clean! . . . Our corrupt condition – by which I mean the aggregation of stupidity, avarice, journalism, business spirit, laziness, selfishness, capriciousness, deceit, hypocrisy and all the rest – hasn't changed at all. . . . The war's great surprise will be in the guns, which are going to show a frivolous generation their utter emptiness. (Berg: 177–8)

Everyone who was touched by this war – and almost no one in Europe was not – was profoundly affected and changed by it. Without a doubt Webern was profoundly moved, but his response was, characteristically, so overwrought and his subsequent actions so indecisive as to appear absurd.

The family was in Klagenfurt with Webern's father when war was declared. In September they returned to Vienna and moved in with Wilhelmine's parents. Webern was subject to be called up at any time; indeed, Berg was called to military service at the end of the month, though he was at first declared unfit. (He was recalled in June of 1915 and accepted.) Webern, with Erwin Stein and Josef Polnauer, took a course in nursing in October and another, in pre-induction military training, in November. Finally able to stand it no longer, Webern volunteered for service in February of 1915.

During the next few months the army imposed on him a life whose restlessness makes it a sort of microcosmic version of the life he had chosen for himself in the years just preceding. At first he was in a regiment in Klagenfurt, but at the end of the first month he was sent to Görz and experienced life in a barracks, though his wife visited him with clean linen and provisions every weekend. Two months later, in early May, he was moved to Windisch Feistritz, where he was billeted privately and promoted to the rank of corporal. In early June he was transferred to Frohnleiten, where he was promoted once again, this time to a rank the equivalent of sergeant, and placed in charge of training recruits. Here he was able to rent living quarters and was joined by his family. In August he was transferred to Niklasdorf and a few weeks later to Leoben. In both of these postings he lived privately with his family in rented quarters. While he was in Leoben, on 17 October, his third child and only son, Peter, was born, in Vienna.

In September of 1915, a year after the impassioned ravings quoted above and after seven months of a life that can hardly be seen as onerous in military – or indeed any other – terms, Webern had tired of the war and of army life. He reasoned that he might be given extended leave if Zemlinsky were to intercede on his behalf, claiming him to be necessary to the operation of the theatre in Prague; there had been, after all, an understanding that he was to take up the job there for the 1914–15 season, though it must be mentioned that this commitment does not appear to have given him much concern until now. But once more Zemlinsky came through, and as a result of his intercession Webern was given leave to take up the position in Prague in mid-December. On 7 November Webern wrote to Zemlinsky, outlining the particulars of his coming release from active duty and asking for a few days to wind up his private affairs in Vienna, as well as inquiring what opera he would be coaching first. He thanks Zemlinsky in ecstatic terms and expresses great joy at the prospect of the coming reunion:

> Ah, I am insanely happy, Mr von Zemlinsky!
> . . . .
> I am very happy that I shall see you so soon, and at last – in Prague.

There are however two sentences near the end of the letter that were more portentous than probably even Zemlinsky, with his previous experience of Webern, could have been expected to recognise:

> It will be beautiful. If only the war were over. *Now again these worries concerning Schoenberg. But it is my hope that things will yet turn out otherwise for him.* (Zem: 285, my emphasis)

Webern is referring to the fact that Schoenberg had been called up on 3 November. During the preceding months Webern had campaigned energetically for Schoenberg's exemption from military service, organising friends to join him in petitioning the authorities in an attempt to prevent Schoenberg's induction on the grounds that it was immoral to ask a person of his obvious worth and singularity to serve in the army. But this immorality was apparently not as self-evident to the authorities as it was to Webern.

The family spent Christmas in Vienna, moving to Prague at the beginning of the new year so that Webern could take up the job there for the first time. No doubt even before he got there he had begun to suffer pangs of remorse that he should have been temporarily exempted from military service while his beloved Schoenberg had, in spite of the protests on his behalf, been called up. Webern immediately set about to get his leave, which had been granted until the end of the theatre season in April, shortened. On 16 January he wrote to Schoenberg:

> I feel like a criminal. . . . It is madness to play theatre now. It is dreadful. . . . In the autumn when I wrote to Zemlinsky, I had such an overpowering longing to be able to occupy myself with music again. And I gave in to that longing. If only I had never done it! (HM: 215)

Later that month Webern's leave was terminated. Again Zemlinsky had no prior knowledge of Webern's intentions; in his innocence he even lodged an official protest at Webern's recall. Early in February Webern returned to his post at Leoben. On 10 February he wrote to Schoenberg:

> I have regrets about my employment in Prague and satisfaction about the fact that I can be a soldier once again. . . . If you must serve, it is impossible for me to do otherwise. (Zem: 285n)

Five days later Webern wrote to Zemlinsky from Leoben, where he had already returned to take up military service, asking Zemlinsky to arrange his release with the director, Teweles, and advising him that it was better to make application through the military command in Graz than the one in Prague, as things would move much more quickly there (Zem: 285–6).

Back in Leoben, Webern again lived with his family, and his duties were light, leaving him time to continue his obsessive campaign for Schoenberg's release. A long letter to Zemlinsky dated 25 February is devoted almost entirely to the subject.

> Yesterday Stein wrote me that the petition for Schoenberg's exemption has been turned down by the Ministry. . . . For what reason I don't know. . . .
> Lehár, the swine, was exempted immediately.
> Not so Arnold Schoenberg. Indeed, how should one understand this, that the great must suffer there as well? And with no distinction, no understanding? (Zem: 286–7)

Webern goes on to say that Stein is going to Karl Kraus. The backing of important people is needed: might Hertzka not be able to do something, or perhaps Alma Mahler? Königer, who was well acquainted with Sylvester, the former president of Parliament, might be able to enlist his help. 'Schoenberg must be set free.' But Schoenberg was not to know of the petition, at least for the moment. On 5 March Webern wrote to Hertzka:

> It is indeed a disgrace that [Schoenberg] was called up at all, whether it was done in ignorance of his personality or in spite of it. To remove such a man from his work is the worst kind of cultural damage the State can inflict. If anyone is 'indispensable' then it is Arnold Schoenberg. (HM: 216)

To Schoenberg himself Webern offered solace, advice on how to get along in a barracks and cigarettes he had handrolled himself. Mixed, inevitably, with complaints. In a letter dated 21 April he described the man with whom he had to work most closely as a 'horrible man, a ruffian altogether impossible to stomach'. Wilhelmine sent provisions to the Schoenberg family.

On 20 October 1916 the labours of Webern and his recruits were finally rewarded: Schoenberg was granted an indefinite leave. Immediately – and predictably – Webern's enthusiasm for serving the 'great, sublime cause' waned once again. His letters are now filled

7 String quartet at Leoben with Webern playing the cello, 1916.

with complaints about army life. On 7 July he had written to
Schoenberg describing the pleasure he derived from working with the
recruits it was his responsibility to train; on 3 December he complains
of disagreeable duties – inspecting uniforms for dirt and missing buttons, supervising in the kitchen, checking on his men during the
night – and of 'being held responsible for everything, simply everything'.

Webern's letters from his army days betray the same lack of per-
spective and control as those from his many short-lived positions
prior to the war. His life was apparently quite a comfortable one:
nearly everywhere he lived privately with his family, in most of his
postings he had very little to do, and in Leoben he played chamber
music regularly with distinguished companions who must have been
interesting people. And, not forgetting the primary purpose of an
army in wartime, it has to be pointed out that he was never in any
danger: he was not ever near where the fighting and dying were going
on. All things considered, one might think that being made to inspect
uniforms for missing buttons and the kitchen for improperly

scrubbed carrots might not have been seen as very onerous tasks. Surely a large number of men holding bayonets in muddy trenches would not have thought them so. But, considering Webern's indecisiveness and ambivalence in relation to what he wanted to be doing and where he wished to be, it is probably just as well that he was not in a position that called for decision-making and assurance.

On 14 November Schoenberg wrote, at the end of a letter to Zemlinsky:

> Right: Webern has just written me. What do you think he wants? You guessed it: to go to Prague. He has been declared *unfit for service at the front*; and Teweles has made him a promise. Is this possible?
> (Zem: 157)

On 23 December Webern received a permanent discharge from military service, having been deemed unfit for service at the front because of short-sightedness. This was the first event to be recorded in Nb6. The entries directly following this one record the family's return to Vienna on New Year's Day of 1917 and the move into their new home there on 12 January. Webern did not go immediately to Prague, but at the beginning of March, on a trip there with Schoenberg to attend a concert, he completed arrangements to start work there in August, and in May the family vacated their flat in Vienna and joined Webern's father's household in Klagenfurt for the summer. On 12 August Webern began work in the theatre in Prague for the second time.

The Weberns travelled to Prague from Klagenfurt via Vienna, where they stayed for a week as guests of the Schoenbergs. This week spent in the same house with Schoenberg, whom Webern had described to Berg on 13 October 1916 as 'someone infinitely sublime', filled him once more with the desire to live in close proximity to his beloved master. On 18 August he wrote to Berg of his desire for a house in the country, next to Schoenberg, and of Schoenberg's idea of founding a colony which would include Berg as well. Schoenberg, as usual, had no money and in addition was subject to recall into the military at any time. His difficulties had the usual effect on Webern, who once again began passionately to mobilise his friends on Schoenberg's behalf. In addition to a personal contribution of 1,000 kronen which he could surely ill afford, he arranged for monthly payments of substantial amounts of money from Alma Mahler, Jalowetz and Stein, and again Königer's wealthy connections were to be tapped. His most ambitious plan from about this time (revealed in a letter to Schoenberg on 22 September) was to use all the money he and his wife had in the world (cash and war bonds, which were very soon to be worth nothing) to buy a farm where he could 'work and do the chores' and grow food for the two families. 'Perhaps it would even be possible for you to live there,' he suggested wistfully.

In September of 1917 Schoenberg was recalled into service, only to be discharged permanently in early December. Now he moved to Mödling, where he was to spend the next eight years. Predictably, Webern wrote, on 7 December: 'When we read that you are moving to Mödling, we had only one thought: we must go there, too. As soon as possible! We are already making plans for it' (HM: 222). One can not help thinking that Webern's use of the first person plural was probably an exaggeration. In any case, this time both Schoenberg and Webern's father expressed alarm at the proposed move. Schoenberg urged Webern to hold on to his job and remain in Prague. In response to Webern's claims that he was being 'exploited' in Prague, Carl von Webern wrote, on 18 March:

> The theatre offers you, after all, the sole possibility of earning! From what else could you and your family live? Schoenberg can really advise you only in regard to your future aspirations, but not about the manner in which you can procure for yourself an assured income, for, alas, he himself has none and has to live off the charity of others. God preserve you from this! (HM: 222)

One can only imagine the elder Webern's reaction to the various activities of his son in the past four months: first his gift of 1,000 kronen to his improvident friend, then his scheme to sink everything he had in a farm mainly for Schoenberg's benefit (in this context it has to be remembered that 'everything he had' had been given to him by his father after the sale of the family estate when he realised that his son had no interest in – or, probably, the business sense required for – maintaining it), and now his decision to give up a job at a time when the whole country was suffering great poverty as a result of a ruinous war. Carl von Webern's reference to Schoenberg makes it fairly clear that Webern must have misrepresented the latter's position in his anxiety to convince his father of the wisdom of his move.

In the end of course neither the advice of Schoenberg nor that of his father had much influence on Webern, although he did, uncharacteristically, finish the season on this occasion. On 2 June Zemlinsky wrote to Schoenberg:

> Webern is coming to Vienna week after next and sends you kind regards. I regret terribly his leaving. But I think his decision to leave the theatre for good is right! (Zem: 195)

Any action on Webern's part that appeared to be decisive must have been welcomed by Zemlinsky after the years of indecision and vacillation he had endured. Webern made only three notebook entries in 1918; these are in the middle of page 2 of Nb6 and record this apparently conclusive action:

14 April 1918	decision taken to leave Prague. Apartment in Mödling rented by telegram
2 May 1918	gave notice to vacate apartment in Prague
beginning of June 1918	moved to Mödling. Neusiedlerstrasse 58

So Webern found himself, with a wife and three young children and with no source of income, in Vienna five months before the end of the war, when the whole country was suffering crippling shortages of food, electricity, fuel and other resources. After seeing him in Vienna on 10 June Berg wrote to his wife, 'Webern, who looks shockingly ill, is already living out at Mödling'. But Webern had obtained the objective he had wanted for so long: he lived only five minutes away from his beloved Schoenberg. On 8 August he wrote to Berg:

I am with Schoenberg daily. I call on him at five o'clock in the afternoon, then we go for walks or we play piano four hands. After supper also we are *always* together. Lately we play card games.[1]
(HM: 223)

The idyll was not to last however. Even before his letter to Berg, Webern had begun to realise that playing cards with Schoenberg was not going to put food on his children's plates. It must have occurred to him almost immediately upon leaving Prague to wonder whether his decision to give up the position there had been unwise; before the summer was over he had asked Jalowetz to make enquiries about the possibility of his return. Understandably he was reluctant to admit this to Schoenberg, who, unaware of the direction in which Webern's financial worries were leading him, was busy making plans for the coming season, plans in which Webern was to play a significant role. Most important of these was the Society for Private Musical Performances, of which Schoenberg, Berg and Webern were to be the central figures. Only in mid-September did Webern finally apprise Schoenberg of his unrest, by way of asking Schoenberg what he thought of the idea of his trying to return to the post in Prague (but neglecting to mention that he had already asked Jalowetz to petition the theatre on his behalf some time earlier). Schoenberg, who had urged him not to leave Prague three months earlier, was furious and replied that he didn't wish to waste any more time discussing Webern's future. On 9 September, after a visit to Vienna, Berg wrote to his wife:

Webern is still at Mürzzuschlag; he seems once more to have rather lost favour with Schoenberg. I gathered this from remarks like 'Webern wants to go to Prague again', and when I looked puzzled and asked what he meant, Schoenberg wouldn't explain. (Berg: 232)

As it turned out a position in Prague was out of the question. Zemlinsky was to write to Schoenberg on 5 November:

The Germans will cave in here, and, with a little 'patience', the theatre as well. And perhaps *very* soon. And then?!? It is altogether

dreadful! The outcome *that* I prophesied, only much more miserable.
. . . Everything thrown over for the Czechoslovakian state! Jews and
Germans, and mainly Jews! (Zem: 201)

The theatre in Prague had replaced Webern and was not in a position
to hire more conductors. Webern now decided to move away from
Mödling (after three months' residence there) in order to remove himself completely from Schoenberg (his reason for moving there in the
first place). In fact the activities of both Webern and Schoenberg in
the next two months resemble those of affronted lovers. Berg supplies
a running commentary in letters to his wife, who was staying at Berg's
family home in the country. On 13 September (Schoenberg's forty-
fourth birthday):

> Webern really *has* fallen into complete disfavour now. . . . Some time
> ago he wrote to Schoenberg that he had more or less decided to go
> back to Prague . . . mainly for financial reasons: his capital would
> soon be exhausted, and he had come to the conclusion that the
> theatre was the right thing for him, etc. I must say that it's madness,
> to my mind, to change one's plans every six months, keep starting
> again from the beginning, and not take into account the immense
> expense of moving house. But as for his purely financial reasons,
> Schoenberg refuses to believe he has only got 16,000 Crowns left
> out of the seventy or eighty thousand he had a year or two ago. (I do
> believe it!)
> . . .
>
>   Schoenberg however, believes Webern has other reasons for
> leaving Mödling, chiefly disappointment at his life with S.—who
> also blames him for being secretive and deceitful. . . .
> . . .
>
> Of course Webern has been a bit inconsistent on several points. . . .
> So S. came to the conclusion: 'Well, perhaps no one can really live
> with *me!*' Now Schoenberg revealed to me the last chapter in the
> story: *Cherchez la femme.* Frau Webern's behaviour has been very
> strange. He believes that *she* is mainly responsible for Webern
> wanting to go. For instance, she didn't have the proper respect for
> S., had taken offence at some of his jokes and answered them with

malicious comments, and altogether may have had an anti-
Schoenberg influence on her husband.

. . .

I couldn't help feeling very sorry for Webern. . . . To condemn Webern
completely I mean, and doubt his friendship, which is really quite
beyond doubt. I can imagine how poor Webern felt on receiving S.'s
answer, saying he couldn't and wouldn't be mixed up in the whole
business any more. (Berg: 235–6)

And three days later, on 16 September:

Well, the most incredible thing has happened! . . . Webern has
broken off his friendship with Schoenberg – simply broken it off with
a few words.

You know Schoenberg wrote to Webern saying he couldn't be
involved in Webern's decisions any longer, as they were always being
changed every six months. I read that shortish letter of his, and it was
rather cool, no doubt, even severe and critical, but not insulting.
After it Webern could either have stuck to his decision and tried to
explain it in more or less detail, or it might even have made him waver
in the decision itself.

But instead he wrote something like this, on a half sheet of
notepaper: 'Dear friend, I am not angry but sad. I would not have
expected it from you, but I cannot change my decision. I shall prove
to you that your efforts for me and advice to me over the years have
not been wasted – if by that time you still wish to know me. The
Prague project has fallen through. I am going to Vienna. Good-bye—
Anton Webern.' What do you say to that? Would you have thought
Webern capable of it? I wouldn't.

Yesterday afternoon when I appeared at the Schoenbergs' . . . he
immediately showed me the letter, then dissected it word by word,
with Tilde assisting: 'Besides being arrogant and uncouth, it's a very
very feeble letter, of course, illogical, unintelligent and smug –
which I never thought Webern was. Must have suddenly gone mad.
I mean, I could have understood his sticking to his decision, but
not his carrying rejection to the point of an actual rupture. Yes, I
dare say it's largely due to a nervous breakdown' – and so on.
(Berg: 237–8)

On 22 September, after another meeting with Schoenberg:

> [Schoenberg] just refused to go on advising him, because, as the facts show, it isn't good giving him any advice. He couldn't go on taking responsibility for Webern's continual changes of mind. He never advised Webern to come to Mödling either . . . [Schoenberg] only sent a very short answer to Webern's long letter, saying he didn't want to be involved in W.'s decision, as he had repeatedly gone into the greatest detail for weeks and weeks over the pros and cons of a change of profession in ten or twenty similar cases – and with some justification he could say: 'To no purpose.' Still, Webern would seem right to look for a secure position at the theatre; though come to that, he has already given up the theatre a dozen times. Anyhow, I wonder how he will fare now in Vienna, what he's likely to expect of *me* . . .
>
> . . .
>
> Schoenberg persists in his severe judgment of W.'s rebuff. . . . Anyhow, the differences have become more acute now after a clumsy letter Frau W. has written to Mathilde. Of course some new details have come to light which help to explain the breach. Among other things some latent anti-semitism in the Weberns, their moodiness and readiness for a quarrel, etc. (Berg: 240–1)

Finally, on 24 September, Berg spoke with Webern and got the other side of the story:

> Yesterday Webern appeared. Difficult to tell you all we said, but the fact is, I now see the whole thing in a different light, and him as on the whole innocent. . . . The reasons for his returning to the theatre were always clear to me. They are purely financial and extremely pressing: he doesn't want to be faced in a year perhaps with complete bankruptcy. . . .
>
> The 'clumsy letter' from his wife to Mathilde which Schoenberg told me about, contained the following, according to Webern. He had promised S. some time ago that he would send him some food from Mürzzuschlag, and when he got hold of this, he couldn't very well keep it for himself despite the rift. So he sent it to Frau S. with a letter from his wife saying: 'After your husband's letter it isn't

possible for us to come to you any more . . . so I am sending herewith the food promised and due to you, which costs so-and-so much': and she gave a detailed account of all the provisions sent. The Schoenbergs returned all the food, *and* the money for food they had been sent earlier, without any covering letter, just the signature, Mathilde Schoenberg. 'Second kick in the teeth,' says Webern.

The funny thing is that Webern of course can't find a flat in Vienna (at the moment he is staying with his mother-in-law) and is today moving back to Mödling! And doesn't know how to avoid any of the Schoenbergs, who of course live very near. He can't imagine meeting S. socially in the foreseeable future. At the idea of it he became quite furious. . . . (Berg: 241–2)

Unable to find anything in Vienna and unwilling to face the problem of trying to avoid meeting the Schoenbergs in Mödling (a dilemma made particularly difficult by what Webern had only three months earlier considered his great good fortune in finding a house right around the corner from them), Webern decided to move to Ettendorf, a village near the Preglhof, between Graz and Klagenfurt. Page 17 of Nb4 contains a list of furniture and household goods to be taken to Ettendorf, along with an itinerary of the trip there, which was to include a stay at Mürzzuschlag.

By the beginning of November, however, the rift was well on the way to being healed, and on 23 November the Society for Private Musical Performances was founded in Vienna, heralding the beginning of three years of carefully rehearsed and dedicated performances of new works without fear of criticism. We shall return to this presently. The Society paid Webern 100 kronen per month as one of its directors; the rent for his apartment in Mödling was 2,000 kronen annually. Clearly there was a significant cash flow discrepancy, and once again Webern's attention turned to Prague. In a letter to Zemlinsky dated 15 June 1920 he refers to an enclosed copy of his contract with Prague which is to his satisfaction and has therefore been signed. He continues:

Please believe me that I am aware of your tremendous patience and your kindly indulgence with me in this matter. And I promise that I

will not disappoint you again; I will see it through this time. (Zem:
292–3)

But in the event, in spite of promises, he decamped once again. At the
top of page 3 of Nb6 is a very short entry: 'end of August – beginning
of October 1920 at the theatre in Prague'. Several factors contributed
to his leaving, but perhaps the most important was the significant
curtailment of non-Czech nationalist productions in the theatre
referred to by Zemlinsky in his letter to Schoenberg on 5 November
1918 (cited above). The theatre was already in Czech hands for three
nights of every week, and things were to get worse. A postcard sent by
Zemlinsky to Schoenberg sometime in November reads:

> I have been in Vienna for six days – on business. In the meantime
> there has been a revolution in Prague; one theatre has been taken
> away from us and I am very curious as to what the outcome will be.
> I will write to you in more detail from Prague. (Zem: 218)

Thus Webern's erratic and unsuccessful first career, as a theatre conductor, after occasioning so much wrath and choler, in the end just
fizzled out.

In the late summer of 1918 Schoenberg told Berg of his wonderful idea
(so Berg described it to Webern in a letter) for the Society for Private
Musical Performances (Verein für musikalische Privataufführungen
in Wien). In November the machinery was set in motion, and on 23
November the Society was officially founded. The Society's *raison d'être*
was to provide a venue for the performance of new works before a private audience from which critics were excluded. It was hoped thus to
produce the best environment possible for an increased knowledge
and understanding of any new music that was felt by the directors of
the Society to be worthy of its attention. In the official Statement of
Aims, Berg listed three things that were felt to be necessary for the
fulfilment of this purpose: 'clear, well-rehearsed performances, frequent repetitions' and performances that were 'removed from the
corrupting influence of publicity'. No signs of either approbation or

disapproval were allowed: no applause, but also none of the hissing, shouting and insults that had been such a familiar element of the concerts of music by Schoenberg and his pupils for nearly a quarter of a century. Expressed aims of the Society were:

- to use 'younger and less well-known artists' whenever possible so as to avoid 'the display of irrelevant virtuosity and individuality';
- to give each work sufficient and thorough study, no matter how many rehearsals this required, and to refuse to perform a work rather than give it an inadequately prepared hearing;
- to provide frequent repetitions of new works;
- not to admit guests ('foreign visitors excepted') or anyone who was not a member of the Society to the performances;
- to obligate members 'to abstain from giving any public report of the performances . . . and especially to write or inspire no criticisms, notices, or discussions of them in periodicals'.

There was to be no announcement, prior to any concert, of what was on the programme, thus assuring equal hearing for every work presented, and no preference was to be shown for any particular school of composition (surely an impossibly idealistic hope). Because of limited funds and resources, orchestral works would be performed in 'good and well-rehearsed four-hand and eight-hand arrangements [at the piano]'. In fact, in attempting to rationalise this latter point, Berg unwittingly shows the unavoidable bias that belies the lack of favouritism avowed earlier:

> But the necessity [of performing piano reduction of orchestral works] becomes a virtue. In this manner it is possible to hear and judge a modern orchestral work divested of all the sound-effects and other sensuous aids that only an orchestra can furnish.

Many a 'modern' composer (the French in particular come to mind) might have argued with this brisk denial of the integral importance of instrumental colour.

Schoenberg was the President and had absolute power. He was assisted by a secretary, a treasurer, an archivist and several musical directors, among them Webern and Berg. In February of 1919 Berg wrote to Erwin Stein that the Society had around 320 members.

The Society met for weekly concerts except in the three months from the middle of June to the middle of September. There seems to be agreement that the first concert was given on 29 December 1918, and that the first eight concerts of the initial season took place on consecutive Sundays from that date to 9 February 1919, though in Nb5 Webern at first gives the dates of these eight concerts as weekly from 12 December to 30 January. In his biography of Schoenberg, Willi Reich claims that from its inception up to the end of 1921, when it was dissolved, the Society gave 117 concerts, at which 154 modern works had been played.[2] Walter Szmolyan lists 113 concerts over the same period.[3] The final concert, a performance of Schoenberg's *Pierrot Lunaire*, was given on 5 December 1921. (This was the fifth performance of this work: it had been presented for the first time on 30 April of that year, and it had then appeared for three consecutive weeks in May.)

During the three years that the Society lasted it kept Webern very busy. As one of the musical directors he was responsible for preparing the performances of twenty-six works in twenty of the thirty-seven concerts given in the Society's first year. He did not appear as a conductor until the second season, when he conducted a performance of his own Op. 10. The Society's policy of performing works for large orchestra in piano reduction meant that a conductor was rarely needed; this performance of the Five Pieces for Orchestra, at the Society's forty-second concert on 30 January 1920, was the first to use one. Webern conducted only one other work, his Op. 6 pieces for orchestra, in the following year. (Both these works were given repeat performances.) The Society's only other conductors were Schoenberg and Erwin Stein. But in addition to rehearsing and conducting, the Society's inner circle were kept busy producing piano reductions of the larger works to be performed. One can imagine that the Society, like the Schoenberg Salka Viertel has described earlier, had the embrace of an octopus.

Webern saw five of his own compositions performed by the Society, all more than once: the Op. 1 Passacaglia was performed three times, both the Op. 3 George songs and the Pieces for Orchestra Op. 10 appeared on two occasions, the Op. 6 orchestral pieces were played five times, the Op. 7 pieces for violin and piano seven.

Schoenberg spent the 1920–1 season in Holland; when he returned to Vienna he seems to have lost interest in the Society. Erwin Stein became director in the autumn of 1921 and, convinced that the Society was not economically feasible as it had been formulated, made the concerts public and instituted advertising. With these changes the Society for Private Musical Performances in essence ceased to exist.

Two of Webern's notebooks, Nb5 and Nb7, are devoted exclusively to the Society for Private Musical Performances. The first, unnumbered, page of Nb5 bears the stamp of the Society, and the date 11 November 1918 appears at the top of page 1; the book covers only the first season (1918–19). The seventh notebook covers only the year 1921: the date 1921 appears, encircled, in the upper lefthand corner of the front cover, and dates in the book run from 23 May to 20 December.

Notebook 9 (see note 2 on p.196) would appear to date from either 1918 or 1919, because page 3 contains a list of gifts that the Weberns intended to give their children for Christmas, and, though there is no date, Christine (who was born on 30 November 1919) is not included in the list.[4] The first two pages of this book contain ideas for eight concert programmes, the first without a date, the rest dated 15, 22 and 29 October and 5, 12, 19 and 25 November. Following the Christmas gift list is a set of eight programmes numbered I to VIII, without dates, which bear very little resemblance to those two pages earlier. All of these consist of combinations and permutations of a basic repertoire, perhaps the works Webern felt able to conduct at this time. This continues for ten more pages. No year is given anywhere, but later in the book the dates 26 November, 3 and 10 December, and finally 1 and 17 November are added. The repertoire that keeps circulating in this book is standard repertoire from Bach to Brahms, one symphony each of Bruckner and Mahler, plus some Mahler songs, Strauss' *Death and Transfiguration*, Debussy's *Prelude to the Afternoon of a Faun*; the only 'modern' Viennese music in the book are ballet pieces by Zemlinsky and a 'Schönberg Sextett', by which Webern must have meant the orchestral version of *Verklärte Nacht*. There is no record of Webern's having conducted these programmes, but they were almost certainly connected to the 'Series B' concerts run by the Society, in which classical repertoire was played.

It is not surprising that the war years and the years of involvement in the Society were not especially productive ones for Webern compositionally. Only four of his works with opus numbers, Opp. 12–15, date from the period between the summers of 1914 and 1922. Both during and after his long and unsuccessful struggle with the cello sonata in 1914 he began to write songs once again, returning to his earliest form of expression. For many years following he concentrated on songwriting, producing only a few unfinished sketches of instrumental music during the years 1914–22, notably four movements for string quartet during the time that he was stationed in Leoben and playing quartets regularly.

The first of the published songs from this period are for voice and piano – the Four Songs of Op. 12, two of which were written in 1915 and two in 1917. The texts are from widely divergent sources – the first is a folksong setting, the others use poems by Li Tai Po (from Hans Bethge's collection *The Chinese Flute*, from which Mahler had taken texts for his *Lied von der Erde*), August Strindberg and Goethe – and are, as might be expected, heterogeneous, ranging from the simple piety of the folksong to the sensuous pleasures of the poem from the Chinese. The musical styles are also disparate accordingly. The only other sketches surviving from 1915 are of two songs on poems of Georg Trakl, a poet who was to occupy Webern exclusively a short time later. No sketches or works exist from 1916.

In the years 1914–22 Webern composed or sketched several songs, all for voice and some combination of instruments – a chamber group of thirteen instruments in the Four Songs Op. 13 on texts by Karl Kraus, Wang Seng Yu (another of the poets from the Bethge volume), Li Tai Po and Georg Trakl; a trio of instruments (clarinet, violin and cello) in the six Trakl Songs Op. 14; and a quintet (flute, bass clarinet, trumpet, harp and viola) in the Five Sacred Songs Op. 15. (The Wang Seng Yu setting of Op. 13 is the only song from these collections to have been written outside this period: it dates from 1913.) Among unfinished sketches from these years are those for settings of two more Chinese poems from the Bethge collection, three poems by Karl Kraus and two by Goethe. Eight further Trakl settings, their dates ranging from 1915 to 1921, were never completed.

During the period when the Society for Private Musical Performances was active Webern made arrangements for piano or chamber groups of his three orchestral works to date (the Op. 1 Passacaglia; Six Pieces, Op. 6, and Five Pieces for Orchestra, Op. 10) as well as music by various other composers for performance in Society concerts, some of which was never performed. Only five original sketches date from 1918, one of these the completed Trakl song from Op. 13, 'Ein Winterabend'. Four more Trakl settings, all later published as part of Op. 14, were written in the following year; apart from these there is only one other sketch from 1919, unfinished, on a text by Karl Kraus. The year 1920 saw only six uncompleted sketches, one for an instrumental trio of clarinet, trumpet and violin, but in 1921, when Webern was occupied with three big arrangements (of other people's work), he also, surprisingly, sketched four more Trakl songs, three of them to the point of completion and later publication.

The four sets of songs from these years show an important progression in Webern's musical style. They came at a time of crisis, when his attempts to rid himself of everything redundant and unnecessary had led him to such an extreme of spareness that there was almost nothing left. Writing for solo voice on a text necessitated a return to longer lines and melodies, greater continuity. The first and second of the Op. 13 songs are fifty-one and thirty-two bars long, making them the longest pieces Webern had written since 1905. They are giants compared with the Op. 11 pieces for cello and piano of only three years earlier. These songs and the Trakl songs of Op. 14 boast a myriad of instrumental effects and instructions for articulation, and both collections are wide ranging registrally, the later work more so than the earlier: in the Trakl songs the singer is required to negotiate a range of over two octaves routinely and the instruments are treated in a similar way, and the dynamic level only rarely rises above pp. In these songs the texture is linear but dense, with rhythmic complexities and sometimes rapidly changing metres combining to produce an ametric effect. Webern described the Trakl songs as 'pretty well the most difficult there are in this field', and at that time he must surely have been right.

During these years Webern's music continued to mirror his life. The longer and more complex Trakl songs, sitting as they do near the end of the period of freely structured atonal music, seem to represent an attempt to find a way out of the black hole of the aphorism, a search for a stability, continuity and discipline that have eluded Webern thus far. These longer pieces coincide with the end of his nomadic days as an unsuccessful theatre conductor and the start of a more settled way of life, beginning with his tenure with the Society for Private Performances. As he was on the brink of a new and welcome method of organising his compositions in 1922, so was he about to begin a new career, one that would bring him satisfaction and recognition. He was about to find maturity on both fronts.

5   1922–8   Changes of direction

I understand the word 'Art' as meaning the faculty of presenting a thought in the clearest, simplest form, that is, the most 'graspable' form.

Webern to Hildegard Jone, 6 August 1928

Three very important things occurred in Webern's life in the decade following the decline of the Society for Private Musical Performances. He enjoyed a conducting career that was, if not very lucrative, more than moderately successful;[1] he began to write music using the twelve-note technique; and he met Hildegard Jone. He also became a teacher, though this career got off to a slow start, since he showed initially a certain ambivalence in this area that is reminiscent of his earlier indecisiveness towards theatre conducting. And these were busy years in terms of his family life: his two younger children entered their teens and his two older ones were reaching their maturity.

The years 1923–31 are the only years of Webern's adult life for which extensive diary entries survive. These are in Nb6; once again the numbering is misleading, as the beginning of this book predates Nb5. Notebook 6 is the most extensive diary of Webern's daily life in existence. It is a different sort of book from the others, a tiny pocket-sized book, beautifully bound in silk with a pattern in purple, yellow and turquoise on a black ground, with the edges of the covers stitched in leather and the page edges gilt. A leather pencil-holder is attached, and all the entries are written in pencil, in a very small hand. This book was obviously carried about with Webern everywhere. It is the only personal diary from his adult life, and though there are entries from 1916 to 1939, those outside the period 1923–31 are very cursory and few in number. The last entry, followed by fourteen blank pages, is Wilhelmine's record of her husband's death in 1945. The book is 106 pages long and covers twenty-four years at a time when Webern's four children were growing up and when his own professional life was busier and more successful than it had been previously or would be ever again. Accounts vary greatly in length.

The records in Nb6 are interesting, both for what is there and for what isn't. Apart from appearances in lists of composers whose works Webern performed during this time, Schoenberg's name appears on only two occasions, Berg's never. Nor is there any mention of the twelve-note method or of the meeting at Schoenberg's house in which it was 'unveiled' – surely a historic event from any point of view. As we have seen, the Weberns and the Schoenbergs lived in houses just around the corner from each other until the autumn of 1925, when the Schoenbergs moved temporarily into the city prior to their departure in January of 1926 to take up residence in Berlin. Numerous members of their circle, as well as Webern's daughters Amalie and Maria, have attested to the physical closeness of this relationship. The two men were together nearly every day, playing endless card games, and, one supposes, talking about music. Maria Halbich has described the horrors of Mathilde Schoenberg's housekeeping and Wilhelmine's occasional visits of mercy to clean the place up. There are many published reminiscences of gatherings at the Schoenberg house, in which various members of the circle took part. Yet from the diary one would know none of this, neither that the two men lived in the same town nor even that they were acquainted. (The only two occasions on which Schoenberg's name appears in Nb6 not as part of a concert programme are in connection with visits to him after he had left Mödling.) Similarly, and just as curious, there is no mention of the occasion in 1926 when Webern met Hildegard Jone, who was to be not only one of his dearest friends and a soulmate for the rest of his life but in a very real sense his muse as well. Her name appears only twice in the diary. The first occasion is on page 84, where Webern records that on 27 June 1930 he was joined in an excursion to the Rax, one of his favourite alpine areas, by the 'Ehepaar Humplik' (Hildegard Jone and her husband, Josef Humplik). A later entry, dated 15 December 1930 (on p. 91), records that Jone had given Webern, after his performance of Mahler's Sixth (on 14 December), her painting 'Der Frühling'. (This painting was one of a set depicting all four seasons, all of which were eventually given by Jone to the Weberns.)

The years covered in this chapter represent a period when Webern seems finally to have come of age. With the return to Mödling from Mürzzuschlag (where he had gone in indignation) in November of 1918 his life became much more stable. Although it is true that his residence there was interrupted on two occasions, neither of these was the result of an altercation or a decision made in haste. The first was the brief period he spent alone in Prague in the autumn of 1920, which, as we have seen, was undertaken because of desperate financial need. The second, longer, absence from Mödling was between 5 January and 5 September 1932, when the family moved house to the district of Hietzing in the city, in the hope of reducing the time Webern had to spend commuting to his numerous obligations in Vienna. This move he recognised immediately as a mistake – he found the street sounds distracting, and he missed the easy access to the countryside that was so important to him.

In 1923 Webern was forty, and as a result of his freely expressed intolerance of anyone who was not up to his standards he had not yet established himself anywhere. Nevertheless he had stayed in place throughout the short existence of the Society for Private Musical Performances, and the new habits seem to have stuck. He took offence no less easily, but now that he lived in the city he loved the occasional contretemps did not result in an immediate change of residence and all the upheavals that this incurs. His growing family would appear to have been an important influence in the settling of Webern; his diary

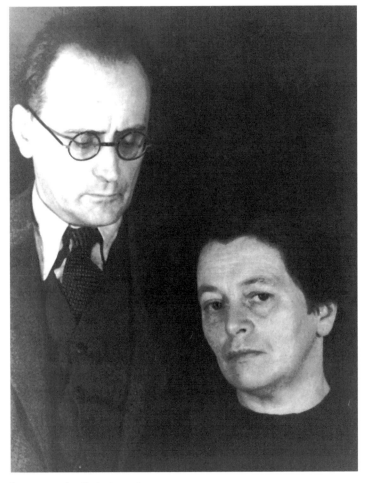

8   Anton and Wilhelmine Webern, 1923.

makes it clear that the details of their day-to-day existence together
were of great importance to him, and this must have given his life a
new dimension and, indeed, a core of stability and happiness that it
had not previously had. In addition, he derived tremendous emotional
and spiritual satisfaction from the alpine excursions, made so easily
from Mödling, in which he indulged whenever he had the time. The

diary leaves no doubt about the importance to Webern of these times in the mountains.

In the eight years during which Webern used this diary regularly, the great majority of entries are of four types: accounts of events and experiences connected with his children, chronicles of his alpine excursions, notices of first performances of his works and a record – and sometimes a report – of nearly all his conducting engagements. It is clear, from the way in which entries are written as well as from their order, that the book was used both as a diary in which to write reminders of future events and as a journal in which to record accounts of things that had already occurred. Only two brief entries refer to current political events: on 1 March 1925 the introduction of the Austrian schilling is recorded (he does not describe the ruinous devaluation that this represented, commenting only 'mayhem in Austria'), and on 24 April 1927, 'Social Democrats won significantly in National Assembly'. There is no other mention of the growing unrest and lunacy that was rapidly enveloping German Europe during these years.

The first things recorded in Nb6 are the dates and places of the birth and death of both Webern's parents (Carl von Webern died on 10 August 1919); the date and place of his parents' wedding and of the birth of Webern's two sisters have been entered here as well. Page 2 contains fourteen brief entries from the years 1916 to 1920. One of these, dated 14 January 1917, records the day that the Weberns' son, Peter, took his first steps. The only entry from 1919 is the birth of 'Christerl' on 30 November.

The Webern children's small rituals and ceremonies are carefully recorded. The removal of Peter's and Amalie's tonsils and adenoids; the first time Amalie travelled to Klagenfurt alone (she was twelve years old), and her return; Peter's first lederhosen. Amalie's trip to Vienna with her grandmother, where they visited the cathedral, the vault in the centre of Vienna where the mortal remains of the Habsburgs are interred, the Hofburg Palace and other famous sights. Wilhelmine's taking the three older children to the Opera to see a puppet show; Amalie and Maria travelling to Mürzzuschlag on 14 July

1925, to be followed by Peter, who travelled there alone on 12 August, and the return of all three together on 20 August. Christine's going to school for the first time, and later her first report card. A haircut for 'M.' (Minna, Mali, Mitzi?). An afternoon outing to the zoo with Wilhelmine and the three younger children. Christmas day 1928, when Christine went ice-skating for the first time.[2]

Official rituals were also faithfully noted. The dates of the children's school opening ceremonies and of the first day of school (not the same, and not the same for all the children) are always noted, as well as the dates of school's closing ('10 July [1926] end of school (holidays: feeling of aimless independence'; 'on 28 [June 1929] end of school. Good reports on the children.'); the dates of the children's first Communion, of their Confirmation (both Amalie and Maria were confirmed at the Stefansdom, in 1926 and 1928 respectively; though the place is not mentioned, Peter and Christine were confirmed together in 1931, and Christine received a gold watch from her grandmother on this occasion) and of their 'Heilige Geistamt' (an event – a Mass at school's opening? – that was recorded for each child in September of the years 1923–6, but which I cannot identify); the dates and results of their school examinations, and observations on the relative value of one school over another; brief records of their individual school outings; and, finally, of their school-leavings – Amalie's in 1930, Maria's in 1931.[3]

Much space is devoted to childhood illnesses (almost exclusively Peter's) and family crises. A considerable portion of pages 11 and 12 describes the death of the family dog. (Maria Halbich says that her father, whose love of plants and alpine flowers is well known, did not much care for animals. Thus one supposes that his unusually long description of the dog's demise probably reflects the important part the animal had played in the lives of his wife and children rather than his own attachment to the dog. There is no record of the Weberns having ever had another pet.) The diary entry, which begins 'Tuesday, 18 March 1924: Peter [who was eight] forlorn' and goes on to explain the reason, traces the history of the dog from the time when he had arrived at the Weberns' home in January 1923 to the end of January 1924, when 'he became ill and very weak', this condition worsening until 2 March. On the 16th the veterinarian pronounced his condition hopeless, and he is described as having been 'very poorly on the nights of the 17th and 18th'. Early in the morning of the 18th the veterinarian advised that the end should be hastened, and the dog died about ten o'clock in the morning. Webern writes that they have

> two pictures of him. One with the children, one with Minna. We thank him for many wonderfully happy hours. I must say that his boundless love and complete devotion to Minna was really beautiful. He followed her faithfully everywhere. And how much joy he gave the others! How gently he played with Christerl. Farewell, dear Pepsi –

The first of several accounts of Peter's indispositions is given three pages in 1928,[4] with an entry every day from 9 to 18 January. Peter, who became ill during the Workers' Symphony Concert conducted by his father on Sunday evening, 8 January, had to spend the evening lying in an armchair in the artists' room and is reported as having been 'out of sorts all the way home, being sick frequently'. The following day he had a high fever, the doctor was called and the source of the trouble was identified as his appendix. On Tuesday the doctor was called urgently at 11.30 a.m. and within a quarter of an hour Peter was in an ambulance being rushed to hospital, where he had an emergency appendectomy between 1.30 and 2.30 p.m. The diary then chronicles the faithful alternation of the Webern parents by the boy's bedside in hospital and every stage of his subsequent progress – changes of room, his first cup of tea, his increasing strength, the return of his temperature to normal, his first food. This saga coincided exactly with the rehearsals for and the first performance of Webern's new String Trio, Op. 20, on 16 January. This concert and its rehearsals are mentioned only incidentally, as things that prevented Webern from being at the bedside of his son, though he does venture to add after the performance that 'it went very well'. On the 18th Peter returned home, and on the 23rd he returned to school.

Perhaps the most space was devoted to Webern's frequent walking trips in the Alps with friends and family. Without question these occasions routinely evoke the longest single entries. The mountains and the alpine flowers there were a consuming passion for him. In the rarefied mountain air, removed from the business of the world, he found the serenity and the mental/emotional equilibrium that seemed to elude him to such an extent the rest of the time. From an early age the mountains had held a mystical attraction and a deep significance for him; letters to Berg and Schoenberg and others of his friends in which he describes the peace and tranquillity he feels in the mountains and his need to go there at frequent intervals are numerous and often quoted. One of his greatest wishes was to share this experience with his two dearest friends; although he writes of his desire to take them into the mountains this apparently never happened.

Webern's alpine excursions were carefully logged. The time of embarking was recorded to the minute, as were the times that all rest stops began and ended, and where they were taken. Weather conditions were always described. And all the wildflowers seen were carefully noted: heather, Turk's cap lilies, alpine chrysanthemums, auricula, black orchis, globe flowers, alpine carnations and, especially, many colours and varieties of gentian, alpine asters and alpine roses (small wild rhododendrons). Occasionally he also mentions finding and gathering currants, and in the description of one visit to the Hochschwab with Minna and the children in July 1924 he records having seen 'many chamois bucks . . . and two marmots (for the first time!)': this is the only time animals are ever mentioned. The mountains he frequented were those southwest of Vienna, between Mödling and Leoben: the Hochschwab, the Bürgeralpe, the Raxalpe, the Schneealpe and the Bürgeralm.

On Easter Monday of 1925 he climbed the Rax alone. His account of this trip, though uncharacteristically brief, can stand as a typical account in capsule form: all the information usually covered is contained in it, but in much greater brevity than is usually the case.

13.IV. Easter Monday, outing to the Rax
(alone)   left Mödling at 6.45
          arrived at Payerbach at 8.25
took the Tärl – route to the Otto-House (about 1.00)
then a bit further on the plateau; same way
back. Left Payerbach at 6.30; home
about 8.45. Beautiful weather. Not much snow; only scattered
on the plateau; very warm. Found
    heather.——[5]

In the years during which excursions were logged in Nb6 five or six such trips are recorded each year. Some of these were one-day or even afternoon outings, walking in the nearby mountains with friends or, more often, his children, but many are extended over several days. The year 1925 is the only exception to this: in that year only three trips are noted, one of which was the Easter Monday outing just cited. The other two were more extended excursions each occupying several pages of the diary.

Alongside chronicles of family events and alpine trips the diary records the facts and dates of Webern's professional life as a conductor, and, occasionally, the progress of his composition. Webern had, of course, conducted his own works on four occasions for the Society for Private Musical Performances, so his ability as a conductor had been observed by those who participated in the Society. He must have made some sort of impression, because his conducting career was launched almost immediately upon the demise of that organisation. Though there are very few entries in Nb6 from the years 1921 and 1922, all but two ('Summer 1921 in Mödling' and 'Summer 1922 in Trauenkirchen') record conducting engagements. In the autumn of 1921 Webern was appointed director of both the Mödling Men's Choral Society (Mödlinger Männergesangverein) and the Vienna Schubert Society (Schubertbund). He was to lead the first of these organisations for nearly five years, but the diary records that he was with the Schubert Society only from September 1921 to February 1922. Though he gives no details, there was some sort of altercation which caused him to announce his resignation at a general meeting called on 24 February. It is clear that his resignation was not unexpected, as his successor was announced at the same meeting. In this event we read echoes of similar difficulties in the past decade. He conducted three concerts with the Schubert Society, one on 9 November and one on 13 February, repeated two days later.

The diary records a Brahms celebration at Eastertime of 1922; Webern conducted the Mödling Men's Choral Society on this occasion, although this fact is not noted in the diary entry. Other conducting engagements recorded in the diary that year are two Workers' Symphony Concerts,[6] on 27 and 29 May, in which Webern conducted Mahler's Third Symphony for the first time; a performance of his Passacaglia which he conducted in Düsseldorf on 5 June; and an engagement to conduct the orchestra of the Vienna Concert Society (Konzertverein) in a series of four trial concerts in September and October with the view of a continuing contract if these were successful.

The morning after the first performance of the Mahler Symphony Berg, who had attended with Erwin Stein, wrote to his wife: 'Last night we had Mahler's Third, and you just can't imagine it. Without exaggeration: Webern is the greatest conductor since Mahler himself, in every respect' (Berg: 301). He goes on to liken the experience to having an injection of adrenaline and says that he was so excited that he nearly forgot to eat that evening. 'I'm almost frightened to hear the performance again tomorrow, that's how shattering it was.' Berg's report of the repeat performance, which was attended also by the Schoenbergs, was just as ecstatic: 'In some respects, it was still more beautiful. . . . Webern's achievement is such that it can only be compared with that of Mahler himself, and such that all doubts, even those of Mathilde, were swept away to be replaced by unreserved admiration' (HM: 245). Berg's insistence on the comparison with Mahler was, of course, the highest praise possible.

After the first of Webern's concerts with the orchestra of the Vienna Concert Society on 24 September, Berg wrote to his wife, once again euphoric:

Webern is the greatest living conductor: the greatest altogether since
Mahler. It's indescribable what he has managed to do in just one
rehearsal. The *Meistersinger* prelude! . . . And Beethoven's Fifth!
Terrific success, completely sold out. (Berg: 304–5)

Fortune must have been smiling on Webern, that in his initial concert
with the orchestra he should be conducting two works that had been
among his greatest loves since boyhood. The third work on the programme was Schubert's Unfinished Symphony. This was a distinguished orchestra, and the position of conductor for this annual
series of concerts would have been a prestigious one for Webern. The
second concert, on 1 October, was, like the first, a success. On this programme Webern conducted Bruckner's Fourth Symphony for the first
time. But then his old nemesis, a combination of uncertain health and
implacability, raised its ugly head. An ear infection prevented his conducting the third concert, on 17 October, even though he had rehearsed
it. When he returned to rehearse the fourth concert, scheduled for 22
October, an incident occurred which caused him to resign forthwith.
He described the affair in a letter to Jalowetz dated 16 November:

> I was just . . . explaining something to the first violins. At this point,
> the first trombonist rose and gave a speech telling me that I was
> wrong, I was *not* in a music school, I was insulting the orchestra with
> every word, that this was no way to rehearse, and that I should go to a
> movie house in order to acquire the necessary routine for myself . . .
> up to this moment the rehearsal had gone perfectly quietly. . . . I
> answered the speech of the trombonist quite calmly and objectively
> and conducted the rehearsal to the end. (HM: 250)

Webern then describes how in the interval a deputation from the
orchestra, including the offending trombonist, came to him and
'tried to conciliate and to *apologise*'. What he says then is interesting:
'But my decision had been made [but not quite, it seems]: *after
consultation with Schoenberg* [my emphasis], I telegraphed the Konzertverein that, because of this incident, I would not conduct the orchestra
any more and that I was cancelling the concerts.' Formal apologies

were subsequently offered by both the Konzertverein and the director-ship of the orchestra. But once offended Webern was ever unforgiv-ing. He tells Jalowetz: 'I could not go on after this all-surpassing rudeness. . . . Alas, these people absolutely do not want to rehearse.' (HM: 250–1)

Webern's propensity for eleventh-hour health crises coupled with the contempt he frequently felt for those he had to work with returned to haunt him several times in the next fifteen years. In view of his obvi-ous talent as a conductor, it seems likely that it was his uncompromis-ing attitude and nervous instability that prevented his becoming one of the really great conductors. His resignation of the hoped-for Konzertverein position in the autumn of 1922 shocked his friends, who had doubtless been encouraged by his landing such a plum. There is no mention of the affair in his diary.

As for composition, there are only so many hours in a day: in the years when Webern flourished as a conductor he had little time to compose. Composition was usually done in the summer, between concert seasons. Because of his heavy commitment to the Society for Private Performances in the early part of 1921 and his subsequent con-ducting appointments later that year and in 1922 he composed very little in these two years. He wrote to Berg on 11 September 1922 that a scandal (of the sort not experienced since the famous Skandalkonzert in Vienna in 1913) that had occurred at a performance of his Op. 5 pieces by the Amar Quartet in Salzburg in August had left him 'out of sorts', and that his summer had not been a productive one. He had almost certainly begun the holiday with high hopes, having been invited to spend the summer with Schoenberg at Trauenkirchen. He wrote the last of his Op. 14 Trakl songs in the summer of 1921 (this song became the first in the set) and, later that summer and in the summer of 1922, four songs which he would combine with one written in 1917 as his Five Sacred Songs, Op. 15. The texts for three of these songs are taken from writings of Peter Rosegger, an author for whom Webern had great admiration,[7] and the other two were chorales, one from Des Knaben Wunderhorn.[8]

More regular diary entries begin in 1923, starting with a performance of the Passacaglia conducted by Franz Schalk in Vienna on 17 February (p. 7) and one of Schubert's E♭ Mass, which was conducted by Webern (though this is not clear from the diary entry) at the local church of St Othmar in Mödling on 13 May, an occasion noted by Webern as 'Mother's 70th birthday!' (p. 4). A Kolisch Concert at the Musikverein on 14 April, in which Webern conducted the first performance of a newly discovered Haydn violin concerto with Rudolf Kolisch as soloist, was not noted in the diary. After this concert Berg wrote to his wife:

> I had been to the Kolisch concert. It was rather nice. Webern got very fine music from the small *ensemble*, and in the artists' room afterwards told me about his present life. He is a nice chap, people are unfair about him. (Berg: 320)

One can only conjecture what the situation must have been that caused Berg to rush to Webern's defence in this way; presumably Webern was still suffering the effects of his sudden – and, it must have seemed to most of those concerned, unwarranted – resignation from the position with the Vienna Concert Society the previous October.

Webern noted in his diary a trip to Berlin for a concert on 6 June[9] in which he conducted his Passacaglia, some Bittner lieder and the first performance of the first and second of Berg's Three Pieces for Orchestra, Op. 6. This concert was part of an Austrian Music Week, and Webern shared the conducting with Steuermann and Zemlinsky. It was a great success. Webern wrote to Schoenberg three times during the few days he spent in Berlin, praising the orchestra as 'grand', 'admirable' and 'indefatigable', regretting that he could not adequately rehearse all three of Berg's pieces in the time given and saying that with Berg's consent he had decided to drop the third piece from the programme.

The diary records two other events in Webern's professional life in December 1923: a concert by the Mödling Men's Choral Society on the 7th and his first rehearsal with the Vienna Choral Society (Singverein) on the 13th. The Choral Society was an amateur choir established by David Josef Bach in 1919 as one of the activities of the Arts Council of the Social Democratic government. It was akin to the Workers' Symphony Concerts in as much as the goal of both was to give ordinary people access to good music, though in the case of the Symphony Concerts it was the audience rather than the performers who were working people. Webern's association with both organisations was to be fruitful professionally as well as satisfying personally, and both offered desperately needed income. His affiliation with both groups continued until they were disbanded when the Social Democratic Party was outlawed in 1934. An important personal benefit of this association was the close and enduring friendship with Bach.

The Vienna Choral Society performed three times during 1924, on 10 April, 4 June and 10 August, the last of these a gala concert in celebration of David Bach's fiftieth birthday. Webern's diary records only two further conducting appearances in that year, both first performances of his own works. On 17 July he began a journey that took him, via Innsbruck, Bregenz, the Bodensee (which necessitated a four-hour boat trip) and Constance, to Donaueschingen for the fourth Donaueschingen Festival.[10] Here he rehearsed his Op. 9 Bagatelles for String Quartet and conducted his Six Songs on Poems of Georg Trakl, Op. 14, for voice and chamber orchestra. On 9 October he conducted the première of his Five Sacred Songs, Op. 15, at the Vienna Secession with members of the Vienna Opera.

The fourth and fifth of the Op. 15 songs are significant as precursors of what was to come. In the first six pages of sketches for the fourth song, 'Mein Weg geht jetzt vorüber', composed in the summer of 1922, Webern wrote out and used a twelve-note row; this was the first occasion on which he had done so. Although the twelve-note version was subsequently abandoned, these sketches show that he was already familiar with the idea at this time. The fifth song, 'Fahr hin, o Seel' (the one dating from 1917) is a double canon in contrary motion, thus looking forward to the intricate canons that characterise most of his later, twelve-note compositions.

Webern's Op. 16 – again songs, and again (like Op. 15) settings of religious texts, this time from the Latin breviary – were all five strict canons. These were written in July and August of 1923 (Webern did no conducting between 6 June and 7 December that year) and October and November of 1924 (the 1924–5 season was a lean one as well – he did no conducting between October and March). The Op. 16 songs were the last of Webern's compositions not to be written with the twelve-note technique in mind.

Schoenberg's famous public announcement of his new compositional technique occurred in February 1923; Schoenberg's reminiscences at the end of his life were contradictory on this matter. On one occasion he claimed to have carefully guarded his secret from Webern until 1923, while on another he said that he was experimenting with twelve-note themes in 1914 and corresponded enthusiastically with Webern on this subject at that time. Schoenberg's first works to be based on twelve-note rows, the piano pieces of Opp. 23 and 25 and the Op. 24 Serenade, were written in the years 1920–3, years in which Webern was occupied with the composition of the Trakl songs (Op. 14) and his two sets of songs on religious texts (Opp. 15 and 16). Webern's sketches for 'Mein Weg geht jetzt vorüber' are proof that Webern knew of the technique at the latest in the summer of 1922, and it is quite likely that he had known about it many years before. As early as 1911 he seems to have been thinking along the lines of twelve-note fields (see his description, admittedly retrospective, quoted on page 77 above, of the way he proceeded when composing the first Op. 9 Bagatelle), and though a sketch of the sort suggested by his remarks about Op. 9/1 does not exist for this piece, a sketch dated April 1914 of a setting of Stefan George's 'Kunfttag III' that was subsequently discarded is very like what he describes there. It contains a list of the twelve notes in which nine have been crossed off, these being the pitches played by the instruments in the final chord while the vocal melody fills in the remaining three.[11]

Schoenberg's statements about the ('his') twelve-note method of composition are not to be altogether trusted. He guarded his rights of ownership jealously. In June 1921 he was one of the judges of a competition for new chamber works held by the Society for Private Musical Performances. This competition was won by a piece entitled *Die Maschine: eine extonale Selbstsatire* written by Fritz Heinrich Klein, a pupil of Berg. On the title page of this work was a list of ideas used in its composition. Among the eight materials listed were:

- a twelve-beat 'rhythmic theme',
- a twelve-different-note 'pattern theme',
- a twelve-different-interval 'interval theme', and
- the largest chord in music: the 'mother chord' consisting of twelve different pitches and also twelve different intervals.

Though Schoenberg was one of the judges it is possible that he did not see this piece, as he was away from Vienna for the summer. A copy of the score found in his library contains the following inscription by Klein:

> It is the same Machine which found itself (as a score for chamber orchestra) in the summer of 1921 in your beloved hands, on the occasion of the competition of the Society f. P. M. P.

With his customary grace Schoenberg added below this inscription:

> Not correct. In Webern's hands, who told me about it but was not able to interest me in it. I doubt if I had this in my hands, but more especially that I looked at it, and certainly that I knew what it represented.

And, just in case the point had not been made, he added, 'In any case, it has fundamentally nothing in common with twelve-note composition' (three quotations from Smith: 194–5). Stuckenschmidt quotes Schoenberg as saying in 1940:

> About 1919 or 1920 Berg brought me a composition of Klein. I think it was called 'Musical Machine' and dealt with twelve tones. I did not pay much attention to it. It did not impress me as music.[12]

On the same occasion of revising history Schoenberg is quoted as having said that he brought his students together in 1924 to explain to them the workings of his new twelve-note technique. Others present at this meeting are in agreement that it occurred in February of 1923. He himself admitted that his only reason for announcing his new method of composition at that time was that he had got wind of Josef Hauer's doing something similar and he was anxious to establish that he had done it first.[13] Hence his constant references to works which he had written in this way as early as 1915. (And his gratuitous complaint that 'After 1915: Webern seems to have used twelve tones in some of his compositions – *without telling me*' (HHS: 442)). It has to be mentioned in this connection that Webern's 'Kunfttag III' sketch dates from 1914, and that Berg had already made use of the twelve-note chord and of chords of fewer notes that complemented the melodies they accompanied by completing the twelve-note field in his *Altenberg Lieder*, written in 1912.

In any case, Webern used the twelve-note technique unequivocally for the first time in the posthumously published *Kinderstück* and the first of the Three Traditional Rhymes, Op. 17, written in the autumn of 1924 (about the same time as the first and fifth songs of Op. 16). In the years 1924–6 Webern wrote six songs, Opp. 17 and 18, and two choruses, Op. 19, all making use of the twelve-note technique. Taken as a whole these works represent a gradual increase in the strictness and sophistication with which he applied the new method; single aspects of the technique are focused on and worked out in turn. In a letter to Berg dated 29 August 1924, just before he began composing the first song of Op. 17, Webern wrote, 'Twelve-note composition is for me now a completely clear procedure.' And so it may have been, though it was not until the Trio for Strings, Op. 20, that he proved his mastery of all its possibilities.

The diary records only three conducting appearances in 1925: the first full evening concerts to be given by the Vienna Choral Society (with orchestra), on 13 and 14 March, and a performance of Bruckner's F minor Mass at the St Othmar Church in Mödling, with Josef Hueber, the Mödling Men's Choral Society and members of the Vienna Folk Opera orchestra. A third concert was given by the Vienna

Choral Society some time in October, but this is not mentioned in the diary. Perhaps not surprisingly, a year in which conducting engagements were so sparse was a fruitful one for composition: the remaining two songs of Op. 17 were written in July, all three of the Op. 18 songs followed in September and October and the first chorus of Op. 19 was begun in December.

There is no record whatever in the diary of an event in October 1925 that was surely of great significance to Webern. In this month Schoenberg left Mödling, thus ending the close proximity the men had known for over seven years. He was asked to succeed Busoni (who had died on 27 June) at the Berlin Academy of the Arts, where he was offered very favourable conditions. Although an appendectomy in November of 1925 prevented him from actually taking up the position until the beginning of 1926, he and his family moved into Vienna in October of 1925 in preparation for their removal to Berlin. None of this is recorded by Webern.

Webern's conducting increased slightly in the following year. There were two Workers' Symphony Concerts, both repeated, the first on 18 and 19 April and the second on 10 and 14 November.[14] The April programme was, as Webern notes in his diary, the 200th Workers' Symphony Concert, and for this occasion he programmed Mahler's Eighth Symphony, the 'Symphony of a Thousand', which required the combined forces of several organisations. Rehearsals went on for months beforehand and the schedule was gruelling. Webern wrote to Schoenberg on 31 March:

> To hold, *almost every evening* for weeks now (after *many hours* of other work), a strenuous choral rehearsal that goes on late into the night, followed by the train ride to Mödling, only then to have supper, etc. – it is usually 2.00 a.m. before I get to bed – this is really quite exhausting. The choruses go at it enthusiastically and indefatigably. (HM: 290)

Nevertheless, Webern lasted the course. The concert was a triumph, even in the eyes of most of the critics. Webern himself was very pleased. In a letter to Schoenberg dated 27 April he wrote:

The orchestra was . . . quite devoted to me this time. It acclaimed me, and individual members expressed themselves very warmly. I may therefore conclude that I have conducted well. (HM: 291)

On 7 May the Mödling Men's Choral Society, with its auxiliary women's chorus, gave a Schubert concert. This was noted by Webern at the end of page 28 of his diary: 'On 7 May, *Schubert Evening*, Mödling, my last concert with the M. M. C. S.' The next entry, at the top of the following page, reads, 'At the beginning of May (1926) resigned my position as chorusmaster of the Mödling Men's Choral Society'. This unexpected event had been the result of Webern's hiring as a last-minute replacement for an ailing soprano soloist (Josef Hueber's sister) a Jew, Greta Wilheim, with whom he was to carry on a friendly correspondence for many years. Josef Hueber has said that the Mödling Men's Choral Society 'had strong German Nationalist leanings' (HM: 292), and evidently these took the form of strong anti-semitic feelings, because most of the members raised an objection to the use of a Jewish singer. Much to his credit, Webern's reaction was to resign immediately from a position which had afforded him considerable personal and artistic satisfaction and, though not princely, by no means unwelcome remuneration.

The only other conducting Webern did in 1926 was at the fourth ISCM festival in Zurich, where on 19 and 23 June he conducted Schoenberg's Op. 26 Quintet for Wind Instruments and the first performance in its original orchestration of his own Op. 10 orchestral pieces. The performances were very successful, even in Webern's eyes, and his orchestral pieces were highly praised by audience, players and critics alike. The whole experience must have been magical for him. The lion's share of his diary account (on pp. 29 and 30) deals with the landscape, the weather and the Alps. He records his arrival in Zurich on 6 June at 7.00 p.m. and the address of his pension. Later he writes that he went via Salzburg and Innsbruck, and that the weather was beautiful, though it rained all the way home. He notes the fact that he had ten rehearsals for the Schoenberg, beginning on 8 June, and seven for his own pieces, beginning on the 11th. But most of the

account is devoted to an all-day motoring excursion into the Alps on
21 June, a 'cloudless day' – apparently a stroke of good luck, as he
notes elsewhere that the weather in Zurich was 'terrible nearly all the
time', with a good view of the Alps on only one day in the entire three
weeks of his visit. He writes briefly, almost as an afterthought, following his description of the mountain trip: 'My pieces performed well.'
His final observation is that there is a fundamental difference
between the eastern Alps (with which he was so familiar) and the
western ones (in Switzerland). Something that curiously gets no
mention whatever in his diary is a reportedly splendid luncheon given
in his honour in which he was introduced to several important people
from the international musical world and was served lobster for the
first time in his life ('How does one eat this? . . . This is really good!'
(HM: 294)).

The first entry from 1927 ('January', at the top of p. 37) records the
first performance of Webern's four Op. 12 songs and a concert (this
was on the 8th) in which he conducted J. S. Bach's Concerto in A minor
for four keyboard instruments (he does not indicate that this programme included also music of Berg and Beethoven and something of
his own). He conducted three Workers' Symphony Concerts that year:
two on consecutive days, 20 and 21 March, to celebrate the centenary
of Beethoven's death, and one on 6 November, on which he programmed Kodály's *Psalmus Hungaricus* and music of Bartók, Liszt and
Tchaikovsky (Webern mentions only the Kodály); the latter was a
celebration of the Republic. An entry on page 38 records the first performance of Berg's Chamber Concerto on 31 March, which Webern
conducted after thirteen rehearsals; this was a concert for the Vienna
chapter of the ISCM. Perhaps the most auspicious conducting
engagement in 1927 was Webern's first invitation to conduct for
Austrian radio, Ravag, on 1 May, the international workers' day. Ravag
was to be an important venue for Webern as a conductor: in the next
eight years, until he was sacked in 1935, he would conduct twenty-two
concerts on Austrian radio, four a year in the peak years of his conducting career, 1930–3. Webern's last concert in 1927 is not men-

tioned in the diary: he conducted the Vienna Choral Society on 9 December at the Hofburg Palace.

Webern's first twelve-note instrumental work, the Op. 20 Trio, was written in 1926 and 1927. It was begun in the summer of 1926, immediately after the completion of the second Op. 19 chorus, at a time when Webern was free from conducting for several months. Apparently however it was finished during a rather tighter schedule in 1927: the movement that was begun in 1926 was completed 'early in the year' and the other movement written only somewhat later, 'in the spring'.[15] This work was a turning point in many ways. Perhaps most importantly it represented a return to instrumental writing after thirteen years in which the only works Webern had felt to be worthy of opus numbers and publication were songs. Although the song had perhaps always been the medium in which he was most at ease, and therefore it is a mistake to see this long period given over exclusively to the production of songs simply as a failure to produce instrumental music, it did nevertheless represent a crisis.[16] During these years (1914–27) Webern had made arrangements of many earlier works, both his own and Schoenberg's, for the practical purpose of making them usable by the Society, and sketched a number of movements for string quartet and trio, as well as the two short piano pieces published posthumously, the *Kinderstücke* of 1924 and *Klavierstücke* of 1925. But as had been the case also with both Schoenberg and Berg, the abandonment of tonality had resulted in an inability to sustain extended forms without the aid of a text; without the tensions and attractions inherent in tonal music decisions concerning continuation and completion – even, to put it rather crudely, of when a piece was over – were largely arbitrary. The twelve-note technique provided a solution to this difficulty, and with the complete adoption of it Webern was able for the first time to write in the forms that had moulded German music for the previous two centuries, albeit in versions considerably tailored to suit the conditions of the new method (for example with aspects of the musical fabric that had been secondary in tonal music now assuming primary functions, structures being determined largely by the reappearance of privileged permutations of the row, and so on). Whereas for the slightly older Schoenberg this step represented a return to the old forms, for Webern it was a beginning; the traditional instrumental forms, while alluded to occasionally in his student years, were not followed rigorously in any of his atonal music. After his adoption of the twelve-note technique, although brevity would remain a cardinal feature of his works, he was to produce no more through-composed aphorisms of only eight or nine bars' length. All the instrumental movements from Op. 20 onwards make reference to the old forms: binary and ternary forms, sonata, rondo, variations, and on occasion – in the Variations for Piano, Op. 27, the first movement of the Op. 28 Quartet and the Variations for Orchestra, Op. 30 – some combination of two or more of these.

The next instrumental work was begun in November of 1927, again not a particularly slack time for Webern, who conducted on 6 November and 9 December. It was finished the following year, when conducting engagements were not numerous. This work was the Symphony, Op. 21, about which more later. On page 45 of his diary Webern records a Workers' Symphony Concert with the Vienna Choral Society on 8 January 1928, at which he conducted the Seventh Symphony of Bruckner for the first time. On 17 April he conducted the first performance of Schoenberg's *Herzgewächse* on a Kolisch-Steuermann Concert that included also a Bach triple concerto and music by Mozart and Debussy. On 1 May, one year after his first Ravag concert, he conducted on Vienna radio a second time. The autumn Workers' Symphony Concert (another celebration of the Republic, this time of the tenth anniversary of the 1918 revolution) was scheduled for two performances, on 11 and 12 November; the programme consisted of Schoenberg's *Friede auf Erden* and Mahler's Second Symphony, which Webern had not conducted before. Rehearsals began in the spring and, as on the occasion of the performance of Mahler's Eighth, performers included the Vienna Choral Society, the Freie Typographia Chorus[17] and the Vienna Symphony Orchestra. But on this occasion, after taking all the rehearsals Webern was forced by illness to pull out of the concerts at the last minute. He was replaced by Erwin Stein. The performances were, notwithstanding, a great success, and this was generally acknowledged to have been Webern's doing.

Webern had been suffering from some sort of stomach trouble since October; an ulcer was suspected but subsequent tests ruled this out. On the advice of friends, and with their financial assistance, he spent 1–20 December 1928 at the Kurhaus Semmering. During this time Erwin Stein conducted a further Workers' Symphony Concert for him, a Schubert celebration. This fact is noted in Webern's diary (p. 59), though the date of the missed concert is not given. The first diary entry for 1929 reads 'resumed my activities in January' and lists these as two sets of rehearsals, of the Bach cantata *Actus Tragicus* with the Vienna Choral Society and of the Brahms German Requiem with the Freie Typographia Chorus. (Both of these works were performed only in 1931.)

Throughout the 1920s Webern had shown an ambivalence towards teaching that recalls his earlier indecisiveness with respect to theatre conducting. In 1920 he refused a teaching position offered him by the Academy in Prague and took over some of Schoenberg's teaching in Vienna instead when Schoenberg spent a prolonged period in the autumn in Holland. During the succeeding years he repeatedly tried to secure university positions in both Vienna and Berlin, and indeed was led at various times to believe that both would be forthcoming, but in the end these hopes came to nothing. When he moved to Vienna in 1918 he did some work as Schoenberg's assistant in his seminars at the Schwarzwald School. A few years later he himself taught a conducting class there, attended mainly by pupils from Schoenberg's seminar in composition. The repertoire focused on Beethoven, and on the anniversary of this composer's birth Webern reportedly told his students that Beethoven's birthday should be observed by all humanity as the most important of holidays. This echoes a letter of 21 December 1911 to Berg in which he had written:

There are few such marvellous events as Christmas. One must consider: after almost 2,000 years, the night when a great man was born is still celebrated by almost all the people on earth as a moment during which everybody says only kind things and wishes to do good to all. This is truly wonderful. Should not Beethoven's birthday be celebrated the same way? (HM: 152)

In 1925 Webern was hired to teach at the Vienna Israelitic Institute for the Blind, the only regular teaching position he was ever to hold, and one that he would retain for six years, during which time his responsibilities and therefore his remuneration were periodically reduced, his accounts book (Nb4) showing a rise from 200 schillings per month in October 1925 to 225 in 1927 and 1928, then a drop to 100 in 1929 and 1930 and a further reduction to 80 schillings per month in 1931, with 300 schillings severance pay recorded in December of that year.

The financial security that Webern's father had hoped to be able to assure for him when he was a young man, first by giving him the Preglhof and later by settling upon him a generous share of the money from the sale of that property when it became obvious that Webern wanted no part in the running of the estate, was to elude Webern for all of his life. The lack of prudence he had shown throughout the decade prior to the Society for Private Musical Performances left him with nothing to fall back upon when the Society went into decline. In 1922 he was thirty-nine years old, with a wife and four children ranging in age from three to eleven years, and neither a source of income nor any savings. Schoenberg, who had earlier benefited greatly from Webern's direct gifts as well as from his tireless money-raising efforts on his behalf, came to his aid. In 1922 and 1923 Schoenberg wrote to wealthy patrons of the arts in Prague, Amsterdam, Winterthur and Geneva on Webern's behalf, begging them to help support the struggling composer. Schoenberg's pleas were rewarded, with the result that Webern was just able to keep body and soul together through the 1920s, though his life was of necessity always very frugal, with his wife selling hand knitting to augment the family income and his children contributing when they were old enough to work. On the occasions when it became necessary for him to spend time at a sanatorium the money was always raised by friends.

In 1924, the last year before the disastrous monetary devaluation in Austria, Webern recorded annual earnings of 72,771,800 kronen. This was worth about £230 in 1924, or approximately £4,060 in 1997 terms. Not much on which to feed and house a family of six. Of this income, 3,000,000 kronen was an honorarium for a performance of the Op. 5 Quartet and the Op. 7 pieces for violin and piano given at the home of Dr Schwarzmann, and 10,000,000 kronen came with the City of Vienna Prize, which was awarded to Webern that year. In 1925 the records show earnings in January and February of 8,009,000 kronen (just over £23, or about £400 in today's terms), 6783.26 schillings (worth about £197, or £3,575 today) for the remaining ten months of the year. The total for September was just over 200 schillings (worth between £5 and £6, £88–£100 today). Payment for the Workers' Symphony Concerts varied from 80 to 120 schillings per month (this went down to 80 schillings per month in 1926) and the Mödling Men's Choral Society paid only 40 schillings per month. When Webern was awarded the Vienna Prize a second time, in 1929, he received 3000 schillings. At that time this was worth just under £87.

Although the length and formal scope of Webern's works changed significantly with his adoption of the twelve-note technique, many features of his style remained much the same. Two traits of his early music that are particularly characteristic of his later style as well are his special fondness for the interval of a semitone in its various guises and his pointillistic scoring, with its resultant kaleidoscopic textures. When writing with a twelve-note row a preponderance of semitones could be assured by building them into the row. The most rigorous example of this is the row for his Op. 20 Trio.

Pointillism[18] is a feature of all Webern's twelve-note works. Typically, lines are divided among several dissimilar instruments playing in widely divergent registers, making linear continuity difficult to apprehend. Thus a music which is already problematic for the hearer because of its dissonant intervals and its concision (material is not repeated or 'played out' in any way) is made even more formidable by its angularity and constant shifts of colour. Webern provided a good introduction to this eccentric type of orchestration (though this was not his purpose) in the arrangement he made in 1934–5 of the Ricercar from Bach's Musical Offering. Here, because the music itself is tonal and conjunct, and, indeed, familiar, the linear connections are easier to apprehend.

Two predispositions that consistently shape Webern's twelve-note writing are his propensity for canon and his fascination with symmetry. These preoccupations converge in the Op. 21 Symphony, composed in 1928. This work is a brilliant tour de force of simultaneous horizontal and vertical symmetries (mirrors and palindromes) unfolding through a series of double canons. Symmetry, like the semitone, could be built into the row itself if desired, as, indeed, it was in the row for the Symphony, in which the second half is the retrograde of the first half at the tritone transposition. The two movements of the Symphony, in ternary sonata and variations forms, exploit various possibilities of expressing these two symmetrical relationships, being all the while in canon as well.

Webern's inclination to conceal is an important factor in the listener's difficulty in coming to terms with his twelve-note music. The form of his twelve-note works is always delineated by the row structure (the return of the same rows in recapitulations and so on), but the musical manifestation of this is so varied as to make aural recognition unlikely. Webern doesn't work with themes and barely with motives, except in the rhythmic sense. Five of his twelve-note works are or have movements in variation form, yet with one exception – his Op. 30 Variations for Orchestra, which is built on two rhythmic motives – none of these movements has a theme (in spite of the fact that he has clearly labelled a theme and its successive variations in the second movement of the Symphony). Paradoxically the themeless variations movement of the Symphony is almost certainly the easiest of his structures to identify aurally because of the careful manipulation of secondary features (tempo, orchestration, density, figuration), his penchant for veiling the truth in these instances serving to hide the absence rather than the presence of traditional content.

I can find no reference to the exact time or place or the circumstances of the meeting of Anton Webern and Hildegard Jone. This is odd, since the significance to Webern of this meeting, which occurred sometime in 1926, cannot be exaggerated.[19] From that moment onwards he set only texts written by her: five of the twelve works written in the years 1926–43 were on Jone texts, the remainder were for instruments only. These five works (comprising sixteen separate songs) stand as a monument to their very special friendship. Jone's poetry is strange and mystical, a sort of introverted latter-day version of the lyrical nature poetry that had so enchanted Webern as a youth. It is filled with references to sounds, with lightness and darkness, spring and images from nature, all translated into human emotions and visions of God. Webern clearly felt a great spiritual kinship with her.

Jone was a painter as well as a poet, and she gave several of her paintings to the Weberns. Only a few of these survived the war. One, entitled 'Roses', which, according to Maria Halbich, hung in the girls' bedroom during their childhood and now hangs in her livingroom, is reproduced as the cover of this book. (This painting later hung in Webern's study in Maria Enzersdorf, as can be seen from Plate 10, on p. 143.) Jone's husband, the sculptor Josef Humplik, made famous busts of both Mahler and Webern, and also one of Webern's daughter Maria, which she still has but will not show because, she says, 'it is at the back of the closet and the nose is chipped'. (I suspect she may not like it.)

In time a voluminous correspondence developed between the Weberns and the Humpliks, an exchange that was continued by Jone and Wilhelmine Webern until the latter's death in 1949. Unfortunately, because of the devastation of Webern's possessions in Maria Enzersdorf in 1945, only those letters written by him to the Humpliks survive. The first of these, to Jone, is dated Christmas 1926 and thanks her for sending him a set of her poems. In this letter he writes:

> In your poems I find again everything that made me esteem your pictures so highly. What it is, is difficult to say. Perhaps one should not try. But one thing must surely be permitted: to say how terrifically pleased I am, after such a brief meeting, to be found worthy of such friendly relations. (Jone: 9)

Thus it would appear that the meeting had probably occurred late in the year and been only passing. On 28 January 1928 Webern thanks Humplik for the Webern bust, which Humplik has given to him, and on 29 December 1929 for the bust of Mahler, with which he has also been presented.

In 1930 Webern writes of his wish that Jone should supply him with a libretto. (This is unexpected, as he had shown no inclination to write an opera since his youth.) This project was soon abandoned in favour of a cantata, though Webern was not to write a work of this sort either for a few years yet. His first Jone settings date from 1933, when he turned from the stalemate he found himself in with the Op. 24 Concerto to write two songs on poems from her *Viae inviae*, the second and third songs of his Op. 23.

On 29 July 1930 he wrote to the Humpliks of a trip he had taken to the Dachstein:

> The day of the ascent there was bad weather, rain and fog, but nevertheless it was very beautiful. The diffused light on the glacier was quite remarkable (caused by the overcast sky and the fog). Just a few paces in front of you snow and fog blended together into a completely undifferentiated screen. You had no idea whether you were going up or down hill. A most favourable opportunity to

contract snow-blindness! But wonderful, like floating in space. And the pastures on the south side! The contrast: luxuriant flora! Nothing but Alpine Roses in full bloom! And lower down the most marvellous Larch woods! Enormous trees growing in the oddest shapes; huge branches. You would have loved it.

Surely a letter to kindred souls.

6   1929–33   The path to new music

> To develop everything else from *one* principal idea! That's the
> strongest unity . . .
>
> Webern, 3 April 1933

Webern's Nb6 continues to record events of his family life in some detail for three more years. In 1929: '*Peter* was ill: 9 February – March (until the beginning of April)'. The next year seems also not to have been a good year for Peter. The first entry for 1930 reads 'Peter ill from 7 to 28 [of January, presumably]. Angina.—' On 3 March a chest x-ray in Vienna showed cloudy spots on Peter's lungs. He was sent to bed on the 8th with a fever, which after about two weeks was replaced by noise in the chest – 'in the lungs and in the heart', according to Webern, who goes on to identify the problem as 'sepsis, just as with Mizerl in January 1927' (this infection suffered earlier by Webern's daughter had received no mention whatever in the diary). Peter went out again for the first time on 2 June. But his troubles were not over. In the autumn (either 3 October or 3 November) he had another fever, and on the 11th of the same month an operation, which was successful, though he had a very high fever (40°) following it. He returned home on the 19th, but suffered a relapse during which Webern writes that he was very near death. His subsequent recovery was rapid.[1]

Purchases are recorded: a bicycle for Maria (who was eighteen) in 1931; another for Amalie (who was twenty) the same year; and, unusu-

ally, something for Webern himself ('Tuesday, 11 August [1931],
bought a typewriter: a Remington tabular portable').[2] His first use of
this new acquisition was to write a letter to Schoenberg, who had used
a typewriter for his correspondence for many years. Schoenberg
responded on 12 September:

> Dear friend, first of all: my heartiest congratulations on your new
> typewriter. An excellent idea that you have decided upon it. It seems
> to be a magnificent machine, which can play all possible 'pieces'.
> Now letter-writing will be a great joy for you! For a while, at least.

The diary stops after the entry for 16 and 17 August 1931, when
an apparently not very satisfactory trip to the Hochschwab was
attempted in 'terrible weather'. It is not resumed until 1937 and is
thereafter used very little, to record only the birth of three grandchildren, the third a stillbirth, in three consecutive years, the receipt of the
score of the Op. 28 String Quartet (from Boosey & Hawkes presumably, though this is not mentioned) and, finally, the flight to Mittersill
in 1945.[3]

Webern's career as a conductor really flourished for only five years,
1929–33. It is impossible to know what he might have achieved had
his progress not been thwarted by the political situation from 1933
onwards. As a consequence of his busy conducting schedule he composed relatively little during these years.

Webern's first public appearance in 1929 was at a concert on 7 April
(repeated one week later) at which he conducted Schoenberg's *Friede
auf Erden* and Mahler's Second Symphony, the programme that illness
had prevented his doing on 11 and 12 November the previous year. He
conducted three Ravag concerts in 1929, on 1 May, 21 July and 20
October. In spite of his busy conducting schedule the first sketches for
the Op. 22 Quartet for clarinet, violin, saxophone and piano are dated
30 May of this year. There appears to have been only one Workers'
Symphony Concert that year: another celebration of the Republic, on
10 November, repeated the following night. Webern's programme for

this concert included Mahler's First Symphony, which he had not conducted before.

It was in 1929 that Webern began to make an international reputation for himself as a conductor. He had conducted his own works at German festivals in 1922 and 1924 as well as his own works and Schoenberg's at the ISCM Festival in Zürich in 1926, so he had had some exposure outside Austria, but in 1929 his horizons broadened considerably. From 15 November to 4 December he made a conducting tour, going first to Germany and then to London, with concerts at the Munich Tonhalle on 19 November, on Frankfurt radio on 24 November and on the BBC on 2 December. Only at the London concert did he conduct one of his own works, the Op. 10 orchestral pieces. Among the other works on these concerts were the 'Jupiter' Symphony, Schoenberg's *Verklärte Nacht*, Hugo Wolf's *Italian Serenade* and the *Kindertotenlieder*.

Pages 68–76 of Nb6 are devoted to an account of this trip. Webern set out on Friday, 15 November, at 11.00 a.m. in the direction of Salzburg. He notes his 'feeling of happiness towards the homeland'; as he leaves Salzburg for Germany he writes 'Farewell to the native soil'. (These feelings of Austria as the homeland and Germany as a foreign land are interesting in view of remarks recorded in 1940: see p. 179 below.) In Munich he was met by a fellow Schoenberg student, Fritz Kaltenborn, with whom he seems to have spent his free time while in that city. The first night was spent in a hotel in a 'very bad district', the rest in the Hotel Eden, which he describes as 'very beautiful'. For his Munich concert he had two rehearsals. The first, on Saturday, he apparently devoted entirely to *Verklärte Nacht*, which he was conducting for the first time; the second was on Tuesday morning, the day of the concert. On Sunday Kaltenborn took him to the cinema to see a 'really awful' film. In a brief appraisal of the concert he found the string playing in Mozart's 'Jupiter' Symphony better in Munich than in Vienna, the performance of *Verklärte Nacht* 'very good', and the orchestra altogether very capable and responsive. He had greatly enjoyed the concert and was particularly surprised and pleased at not having experienced any hint of nervousness. Afterwards he and Kaltenborn ate well at the Hotel Deutscher Kaiser. In summing up the visit he describes his stay in Munich as an altogether very pleasant experience, says he had an excellent rapport with the orchestra and reiterates a view he had long held of Munich as a beautiful city and Bavaria a fine province. And, as always, he records the weather: 'snow was falling between Salzburg and Munich' and there was 'winter weather in Munich' itself, 'clear and frosty'.

In Frankfurt, the next stop on his journey, he was met by Adorno,[4] who took him to the home of Dr Milton Seligmann, a high court judge and amateur musician one of whose sons was a pupil of Schoenberg. During his stay in Frankfurt Webern was the Seligmanns' houseguest, and he writes that he was 'put up wonderfully and lived really magnificently'. He had two days to look around the city (and study his scores) before his first rehearsal; he writes that, sadly, he did not see the Goethe house. He had lunch with Adorno on Friday and that evening rehearsed the *Kindertotenlieder*, which he was conducting for the first time, with his friend Hueber, who had arrived that day from Vienna. He had two orchestral rehearsals, on Saturday and Sunday; the concert was on Sunday evening. After the first rehearsal he writes that the orchestra is good, a few of the winds particularly so, and that good rapport was achieved quickly. His report of the concert is similar to his report of the concert in Munich. Everything went 'very well', the Mozart (this time a divertimento) better than in Vienna.

The following morning Webern was off to Cologne for a three-day visit with his old friends Heinrich and Johanna Jalowetz. They made good use of their few days together, taking in a concert, a film and the opera (where Jalowetz now conducted). Webern sums up Cologne as 'a splendid city, very lively' and writes of the 'great joy' of seeing Jalowetz again at last. (Webern must have found his visits to Frankfurt and Cologne wonderfully distracting, because for over a week he did not mention the weather.)

Finally, on Thursday, 28 November, at 6.45 a.m., Webern began his difficult journey to England. His trip took him through Aachen to

Ostende. In spite of the fact that it was raining and dreary, he writes of the wonderful impression he got of Brussels from the train. He says the architecture of the city is essentially German. After lunch in Ostende he boarded the boat at 3.30 in the afternoon for the journey to England, which took four and a half hours. At first he was on deck, then he slept for two hours below, only to be awakened by a storm that sent him rushing back on deck, where he stood for two hours, watching. 'The sea raging. Waves the height of a house. In a wretched state, but held fast.' About 10.30 p.m. he arrived at last in London, where he was awaited by Edward Clark, a Schoenberg pupil from Webern's days in Berlin who was now with the BBC and was responsible for arranging Webern's London engagement. Clark took him to his hotel, the Strand Palace, and then to a party. Webern declares, understandably, that by this time he was very tired.

The following morning, Friday, Webern had the first rehearsal of his Op. 10 orchestra pieces. His comment 'Little understanding on the part of the orchestra' may refer either to their lack of understanding of the piece or, more likely, to the fact that they found it very difficult to understand Webern himself and what he wanted of them. He writes that the orchestra is excellent. He had a second rehearsal the following day and a third on Monday. Most of the rest of the time was spent with Clark, who showed him the sights of London and took him to his first sound motion picture, which he 'liked very much!'. The radio concert, on Monday evening, was in front of an audience in a theatre, a situation that he found a bit unsettling. He writes that the performance of his own pieces was excellent, but he was not very happy with the way either of the other two works on the programme (Milhaud and Brahms) was played. His Op. 10 was repeated for the theatre audience after the broadcast was over. The performance was followed by a short party, then dinner at a restaurant. The next morning (Tuesday, 3 December) he was on his way home. This time the crossing was smooth, and, after a short visit with the Jalowetzes between trains in Cologne (at 1.00 a.m.!), he arrived back in Vienna at 9.30 in the evening on Wednesday, where he was met at the station by

Wilhelmine and the two younger children. He declared himself to be indescribably happy to be home again. Reflecting on his first visit to London, he writes that he was 'not very enchanted' with it. The first thing that comes to his mind is the 'colossal traffic'. But as he goes on and thinks about it longer, London gets worse and worse. He writes of finding both the orchestra and Clark (who had put Webern up in quite a decent hotel and devoted practically all of his time to him during his visit) unsympathetic, as, indeed was the 'entire nature of things'. He could scarcely wait to get away from the parties, which he found unbearable. He had hated the sea, the crossing, the coast, the fog, the gloom; while he was there he had longed for the mountains and the flowers, for blue skies and clear air. He had been 'truly disappointed'. One cannot help wondering why he repeated such an arduous and unrewarding journey on five subsequent occasions. As an after-thought he says that he had felt well and that the weather was good.

On 14 December, ten days after his return to Vienna, Webern conducted a Steuermann-Kolisch Concert in Vienna with orchestra and chorus (the Vienna Choral Society) in which Hueber and Steuermann were soloists. Early the next morning he travelled to Berlin, where he was to conduct a radio concert on the 18th.

Webern's record of this journey differs markedly from those of his recent visit to London. But of course he was back in Germany. And, even more, he was in Berlin, where Schoenberg now lived. This very same personage met him upon arrival, and he stayed in the Schoenbergs' home. ('Lovely, beautiful hours.') On both Monday and Tuesday the morning was spent rehearsing, the afternoon and evening in the company of Schoenberg. Wednesday morning was spent at home with Schoenberg, Wednesday afternoon in the city with Schoenberg. The concert was that evening at 7.30. On the programme were Beethoven, Brahms, a Mozart concerto with Steuermann as soloist and Webern's Passacaglia. In his assessment of the performance Webern writes that the Beethoven (the *Coriolan* Overture) was 'not very good', the Brahms (Serenade, Op. 6) 'better than in either Vienna or London but under-rehearsed' ('The lovely, sweet sound that I wanted did not happen here either'), the Mozart 'good' and the Passacaglia largely all right. Of the last he says he is very happy with the work itself, but that it is a difficult piece and requires much rehearsal. Thursday afternoon was spent with Schoenberg, and that evening Webern began the return journey to Vienna, where Wilhelmine met him at the station the following day.

Webern did not conduct outside Vienna in 1930 but had a full schedule nevertheless. His first appearance that year, on 24 February, was at a Steuermann-Kolisch Concert at which his new Symphony, Op. 21, received its first performance (the diary entry, on p. 77, reads 'Great delight. Turned out really well.'). A second Steuermann-Kolisch Concert on 5 March consisted of two Schoenberg works (the First String Quartet and the Op. 29 Septet, the first Viennese performance of the latter) and the third Brandenburg Concerto.[5] His first Ravag concert of the year followed only five days later, with a completely different programme, including a Beethoven symphony, and on 16 March he conducted the first Workers' Symphony Concert of the year in a programme that included none of the works from the previous concerts. It would seem that Webern had finally built up some stamina: his schedule for the winter and spring of 1930 was unusually taxing, and he didn't buckle under it. He conducted four Ravag concerts (on 9 March, 1 May, 22 June and 10 November), these programmes including, among other things, the Adagietto from Mahler's Fifth Symphony; two Mozart symphonies and the Concerto for Flute, Harp and Orchestra; the Third, Seventh and Eighth Symphonies of Beethoven and the *Consecration of the House* Overture; Schubert's Fifth Symphony; Brahms' *Tragic* Overture and Webern's own Passacaglia for Orchestra. His diary records on page 77 that the Passacaglia was performed much less well than it had been in Berlin, as the result of having been 'quite insufficiently rehearsed'. As usual, there were no summer engagements; after a Ravag concert on 22 June he was free until 10 November. During this time he finished the Op. 22 Quartet. A Vienna Choral Society concert in Hietzing on 28 November is noted in the diary, as are a concert in honour of Karl Renner, the first

Chancellor of the Austrian Republic, on 13 December (not, apparently, a Workers' Symphony Concert, in spite of its Republican theme)
and a Workers' Symphony Concert the following evening. On the
latter occasion Webern conducted Mahler's Sixth Symphony for the
first time.

Conducting engagements were slightly less numerous in 1931,
though Webern travelled abroad to London again. In Vienna he conducted three Ravag concerts (on 4 January, 29 March and 1 May); and a
performance of the German Requiem at a Workers' Symphony
Concert, which was broadcast as well, on 12 April. On 5 May he left for
London, where he conducted two BBC concerts, one with traditional
repertoire on 7 May, the other, on the following day, devoted entirely
to his own music and that of Schoenberg. Diary entries for this trip are
cursory compared to those of his visit to London two years earlier.
Again he travelled via Cologne and visited the Jalowetzes.

A historic event is recorded on pages 99–100 of Nb6: the first
recording ever conducted by Webern, two Ultraphon records, one of
songs by Brahms and Schoenberg, the other of songs by Eisler. This
was done in Mödling and formed part of a recorded series of Austrian
music. Illness struck again late in 1931, however, making it impossible for Webern to conduct a fourth scheduled Ravag concert which
was also the second Workers' Symphony Concert for the year. As
before, he persevered with rehearsals until the eleventh hour. On 31
October he took the last rehearsal of the concert, which was on the following day, and he did not inform his friend Bach that he was too ill to
take the concert until a few hours before it was to begin. Two conductors were enlisted at literally the last moment, and the show went on.
This concert was the occasion of a political storm in the press. The
controversy was over the inclusion of Bach's *Actus Tragicus* on the programme, since any modicum of religious content in a Workers'
Symphony Concert was seen by some socialist supporters as unacceptable. The same group favoured the introduction of new music
on these programmes, and the situation was complicated on this
occasion by the fact that Webern had declined to perform a new choral

work by Rudolf Réti (his stated reason being that it was too difficult and his choir refused to sing it) and appeared to be performing the Bach in its place. The day after the concert *Der Morgen* ran a headline 'Nervous Collapse of Anton Webern before Yesterday's Workers' Concert' and went on to imply that Webern had failed to appear on that occasion because of the controversy surrounding the programming of the Bach cantata. A second newspaper some days later admitted, after an interview with Webern's wife, that Webern was in fact quite ill. In retrospect, both were probably right. Webern's problem was the same as before – severe stomach difficulty of some sort, though not ulcers – and one has to suppose that the condition was probably not helped by all the uproar surrounding the concert. On 14 November Webern again entered a sanatorium, this time the Sulz-Stangen Sanatorium near Hinterbühl, close to Mödling. He had recovered sufficiently to return home at the beginning of December.

Webern did more conducting in 1932 than in any year so far. Again he had the usual four engagements with Ravag (on 31 January, 1 May, 16 October and 1 November), and the customary two Workers' Symphony Concerts (on 13 March and 26 November). One week after the first of these, which was in celebration of the centenary of Goethe's death and consisted solely of works on Goethe texts, he conducted a second concert in celebration of the Goethe centenary, in which the Vienna Symphony Orchestra played Wagner's *Faust* Overture. On 21 February he conducted a concert of American music for the Pan American Association of Composers. This was all music he had not conducted before.

On 1 April Webern and Steuermann left for Barcelona, where Schoenberg had been living since the previous autumn. Schoenberg had arranged two concerts for Webern there, with the Pablo Casals Orchestra. On 3 April they heard Schoenberg conduct his *Pelleas und Melisande*, and Webern then conducted concerts on 5 and 7 April. At the first of these, in addition to the 'Clock' Symphony of Haydn and Beethoven's Seventh Symphony, Webern conducted three of his own works: his orchestration of Schubert German Dances, his Op. 6 pieces for orchestra and the Passacaglia. The second programme included his first performance of Mahler's Fourth Symphony (a work about which he had declared in 1913, 'as with all works of such an elevated nature, . . . this is dictated'). Less than two weeks later Webern travelled to Frankfurt for a radio broadcast on 21 April that included his Op. 14 Trakl songs and his Symphony. On 29 December he returned to Frankfurt for a second radio concert.

The tenth ISCM Festival was held in Vienna in 1932. Webern conducted on 16, 19 and 21 June. The concerts were grand successes, acclaimed in Vienna and elsewhere. Schoenberg wrote from Barcelona saying that he had heard wonderful things about Webern's performance at the Vienna ISCM Festival. Webern, however, fainted during the final rehearsal for the third concert and, though he made it through the concert this time, was sent to hospital immediately after. The diagnosis was essentially the same as it had always been: the basis of his stomach difficulties was not organic but nervous. This time he was ordered to take a long cure; again this was paid for by friends. He went from one hospital to another, complaining bitterly that his one opportunity to compose that year – the summer – had to be wasted in this fashion. He wound up however at Bad Fusch, in the midst of the high mountains that he so loved, which must have been about as near to paradise as he ever got. He wrote ecstatically to Schoenberg that he could see the glaciers of the Hohe Tauern every day and that he felt rejuvenated in this atmosphere. He returned home on 28 August, just in time to help his family move from their city apartment in Hietzing to the house at Im Auholz 8 in Maria Enzersdorf on 5 September (see p.105 above).

In 1933 Webern made his third trip to London to conduct for the BBC. He gave two concerts there, on 21 and 23 April. Among the works on the programmes were the Mahler Fourth and two works by Berg, his Chamber Concerto and two movements of the orchestrated *Lyric Suite*. Webern wrote to Schoenberg on 3 May:

9 Webern in his garden in Maria Enzersdorf, 1933.

I believe that Berg's works turned out very well, at any rate they were clean throughout. They also met with great success. . . . *The orchestra is really splendid.* How they played Mahler's Fourth! . . . I might also report in all modesty that, from all appearances, I have had a very far-reaching effect on the orchestra (acclamations during and at the

10 Webern photographed by Hildegard Jone in his study in Maria Enzersdorf,
1940.

end of the rehearsals, a spontaneous storm of applause after the
Prometheus Overture, and after the second concert a veritable ovation).
In short, dearest friend, I was really very, very happy. (HM: 396–7)

Back home, Webern conducted his usual four Ravag concerts (on
23 May, 21 July, 28 September and 6 November). No new repertoire

was included in the first two of these, but he conducted Beethoven's Triple Concerto (with Kolisch, Steuermann and Benar Heifetz) and Brahms' Fourth Symphony, both for the first time, on the third. Besides these broadcasts he conducted his usual two Workers' Symphony Concerts, on 19 March and 10 December. The first of these, in commemoration of the March 1848 uprising in Vienna, was entirely devoted to contemporary German/Austrian music – works by Krenek, Paul Pisk and Eisler. The second, a celebration of Webern's tenth anniversary with the Vienna Choral Society, contained only the work of older Viennese composers (Beethoven, Mozart, Brahms and Schubert). Webern was not to know that this was to be both the last appearance of the Choral Society and the last Workers' Symphony Concert.

Webern's conducting repertoire included the first eight Beethoven symphonies (his first performances of these spanned ten years, from September 1922, when he conducted the Fifth for the first time, to October 1932, when he first conducted the First; he conducted the 'Eroica', the Seventh and the Eighth all for the first time in 1930). The Ninth, which he had loved from his youth, he never conducted, though Moldenhauer says that he rehearsed it in 1933 but could not get it ready in time (HM: 401). In October of 1922 illness prevented his conducting the Brahms First Symphony, which he had rehearsed, and he succeeded in conducting the Fourth eleven years later; he apparently never did either the Second or the Third. Of the Bruckner symphonies he conducted only the Fourth and the Seventh; of Mahler's symphonies, the first six and the Eighth, but only two movements (on separate occasions) of the Seventh. He never conducted the Ninth, in spite of his great admiration for it (in a letter to Schoenberg in 1912, after playing through the score with Jalowetz, he had called it 'inexpressibly beautiful'; two years later he wrote 'It is really like a greeting from above. Mahler then was already far, far away from us' (HM: 160, 128)). He conducted six of Mozart's forty-one symphonies, including the 'Jupiter', and Schubert's Fourth, Fifth, Seventh and Eighth, but only one symphony each by Haydn and Mendelssohn, and only the Second Symphony of Schumann, in Mahler's version.

In 1929 Schoenberg was asked to lecture at the Austro-American Conservatory at Mondsee near Salzburg and he requested that Webern be hired to give an introductory course as a preparation for his lectures. This prospect pleased Webern, and he prepared a course carefully, often asking Schoenberg's advice. He was very disappointed when the whole thing fell through at the last minute. In 1932 he was encouraged to give these lectures privately in the home of Dr Rudolph Kurzmann, and thus began a series that continued until the last months of the war. The first two of these sets of lectures were taken down in shorthand by Webern's friend Dr Rudolf Ploderer and later transcribed by Willi Reich and published as *The Path to Twelve-note Composition* (the series of weekly lectures given between 15 January and 2 March 1932) and *The Path to the New Music* (the series given between 20 February and 10 April 1933) and in this form have taken their place in the canon of writings about the history of chromatic atonal and twelve-note music. Succeeding series of lectures dealt with the study of traditional structures, through analysis of the works of Beethoven and other German masters. (Many of these were taken down in shorthand also, by a second pupil, Siegfried Oehlgiesser, and should be published in the near future.) In his youth Webern had written in his diary, 'The genius of Beethoven reveals itself more and more clearly to me. It gives me an elevated strength . . . and one day the moment will come when I am directly imbued, in brightest purity, with his divinity. He is the comfort of my soul . . .'. This admiration for Beethoven now took a more clearly defined and specific form. Webern's belief in the significance of Beethoven in the history of music was lifelong and unswerving.

Webern began writing his large instrumental works ('large' in concept, never so in terms of real time) at a time when he was becoming established as a conductor, so progress was slow. In the year 1929, for instance, when his career as a conductor began to gain momentum, with eleven concerts, in Munich, Frankfurt, London and Berlin as well as Vienna, he produced, as we have seen, no compositions at all. In the following year, which saw as much conducting as 1929, he finished a single work, the Op. 22 Quartet, which he had begun the previous year. On 16 January 1931 he began sketching his third major instrumental work, the Op. 24 Concerto for Nine Instruments. This work was to give him a great deal of difficulty. He came to an impasse with the first movement, and its composition occupied him on and off for the next three years. He produced nothing in either 1931 or 1932 (both busy conducting years). On 1 February 1933 he turned once again to song-writing as he had done before in times of compositional crisis, composing two of the three songs of Op. 23 in the summer of that year.

The hiatus that Webern suffered in his composition of Op. 24 resulted from the unforeseen difficulties inherent in a row with a particular kind of symmetry. His row for this work was inspired by a Latin acrostic (see Figure 1)[6] which can be read in four directions. He constructed a row that very closely approximated the symmetry of this acrostic. Having done this he then encountered the problem of producing the variety necessary to sustain interest while at the same time retaining the integrity of the row. In Webern's exploration of symmetrical possibilities the Op. 24 Concerto represents an extreme in its concern with microcosmic detail.

Figure 1

```
S A T O R
A R E P O
T E N E T
O P E R A
R O T A S
```

One of the most important fundamentals of Schoenberg's teaching was the necessity for unity. He explained this endlessly as the synthesis of the horizontal and the vertical, something that was in his view ensured by the proper use of twelve-note rows as the basis of composition. This idea of synthesis was carried out relentlessly by his one-time pupil. Webern felt that he had found a very significant analogue in the *Urpflanze*, Goethe's concept of a plant as a single substance, in which stem and leaf and blossom are all manifestations of the same fundamental element. He must have thought that he had found a perfect musical parallel when he built this twelve-note row.

While Webern was puzzling over ways to control his super-symmetrical row things were going badly awry in Germany and surrounding Europe. Hitler and the National Socialists seized power in Germany effectively in January of 1933, though Hitler became dictator by official sanction of the Reichstag only on 23 March. The Communist Party was immediately outlawed in Germany. The 'purification' of culture began in earnest in Germany even before Hitler's official enthronement. Webern, who as we shall see for many years refused to recognise the reality of the horrors perpetrated by the German National Socialists, remarked nevertheless in his *Path to the New Music* lecture on 14 March 1933, 'What's going on in Germany at the moment amounts to the destruction of spiritual life!' But of course things were to get very much worse.

7   1933–8   Before the Anschluß

All art, all music is based on laws.

Webern, 14 December 1934

On 3 December 1933 Webern was fifty. His friend David Josef Bach was instrumental in organising a celebration, under the auspices of the local chapter of the ISCM, in the little hall of the Musikverein on 2 December which Webern later described to Schoenberg with the greatest pleasure. (He felt it necessary to apologise for his delight: 'Do not be cross with me because I tell you this. I only want to report to you how it was.') Maria Halbich remembers this concert also as a great occasion for her father, and for his whole family. There was an address by Bach, to open a celebratory concert of Webern's music;[1] a dinner that followed at a restaurant was attended by various dignitaries. Jalowetz, Adorno and others wrote newspaper articles about Webern, and further performances of his music occurred on 1, 3 and 5 December (the first of these on the BBC: Webern reports wryly to Schoenberg that he 'could even hear a little of it'). There were other performances, in Winterthur and Prague. A special issue of the journal 23 was devoted entirely to Webern. Berg dedicated his just completed 'Lied der Lulu' to Webern (fifty bars – appropriately – which Berg described as 'perhaps the most important of the entire opera'). In addition there was a private celebration, at the home of Mark Brunswick, a composer from New York who was known for his lavish

148

entertaining. This occasion was a surprise party, and after dinner with several of his close friends, Webern was treated to another performance, this time of his pieces for string quartet, Opp. 5 and 9, played by the Galimir Quartet. There was only one sour note: a Professorship that he had been led to expect on this occasion, a project which had been enthusiastically pursued by Alma Mahler and others of his friends, failed to materialise.

As it happened, these joyful celebrations coincided with the beginning of the very rapid decline of Webern's fortunes. Coming at the end of 1933 the revelling must have struck many as hollow, though it is very likely that Webern himself was immune to this perception. 1933 had not been a good year, and it was only the beginning. Immediately upon their coming to power in Germany the National Socialists had begun their programme for the 'purification' of the arts. On 11 March several leading figures in the arts in Germany were dismissed for being Jewish or in some other way 'impure'. Goebbels, who was at this time Hitler's minister of Volksaufklärung (Popular Enlightenment) and who would in November become the head of the Reichsmusikkammer (National Ministry of Music), put a stop to all radio broadcasts of American jazz and cancelled concerts that were scheduled to be led by Jewish conductors. A protest from a group of eminent American musicians resulted in their music being proscribed as well. In Berlin, Schoenberg walked out of a meeting of the Senate Council of the Berlin Academy on 1 March when new regulations were read out demanding a halt to Jewish influence at that institution. He submitted his letter of resignation on 20 March. In May he and his second wife and baby daughter left Germany, going first to Paris, then to Arcachon near Bordeaux, and finally, in October, to the United States.[2] It is a measure of Webern's lack of perception about what was happening that he tried urgently to persuade Schoenberg to return to Vienna. The emigration of his dearest friend and teacher was a terrible blow for Webern. It was not his first loss, and it certainly would not be his last.

One of Webern's friends from university days and a fellow Schoenberg pupil, Karl Horwitz, had died an untimely death from the aftermath of tuberculosis in 1925. Emil Hertzka, the director of Universal Edition, who had been a loyal friend to Webern and a champion of the music of the new Viennese school, and who had published all of Webern's works with opus numbers (with the exception of the Op. 6 orchestral pieces, which Webern had published privately) and arranged for a small regular income for Webern as well, died in 1932. Another of Webern's close friends, Rudolf Ploderer, committed suicide in September 1933. Only a month earlier the famous Bauhaus architect Adolf Loos had died after a long illness. (In his diary Webern had recorded a visit to Loos with Schoenberg on 20 October 1930, when they found him 'very ill'. Webern had dedicated his Op. 22 Quartet to Loos on the occasion of his sixtieth birthday on 10 December of the same year.) Already old friends had begun to disappear. Now, with the Nazis' 'purification' campaign, other friends began to vanish for other reasons. Adorno emigrated to Oxford in 1934 and from there to New York four years later. Kolisch moved to the US in 1935, Eduard Steuermann, Friedrich Deutsch (a Webern student who changed his name to Frederick Dorian when he emigrated) and Paul Pisk followed suit in 1936, Ernst Krenek in 1937. Most of Webern's American students began to return home about the same time. Moldenhauer relates an episode recounted to him by Felix Galimir:

> Dr Bach at one point became very critical of the Germans' attitude towards the Jews. At that point Webern interrupted him: 'But David, not all Germans are Nazis!' Thereupon Dr Bach closed the discussion with the words: 'Every German who has not given absolute proof to the contrary is a Nazi.' (HM: 473)

Webern, who believed so fervently in the superiority of German culture, never gave that proof.

In March, as Hitler became ensconced in neighbouring Germany, the Austrian Chancellor, Engelbert Dollfuss, had suspended the parliamentary constitution and established an authoritarian government in Austria. An uprising by the Social Democratic Party in

February 1934 led to rioting in the streets and left a thousand people dead and three to four thousand wounded. As a result of this both the Social Democratic Party and the National Socialist Party were outlawed in Austria. With the SDP went its various cultural organisations, among them the Vienna Choral Society and the Workers' Symphony Concerts.

Webern conducted only once in Vienna in 1934. On 28 January he conducted a programme of Mendelssohn (probably not a fortuitous choice, under the circumstances) for Ravag in celebration of that composer's birthday. He was not asked to conduct another Ravag concert that year. He conducted only once more in 1934, travelling to England for a single BBC concert on 25 April.

The virtual end of his conducting career in 1934 (it was to end in fact two years later) meant of course that, though Webern had less money, he had more time to compose. He wrote the third of the Op. 23 songs in January–March, and he finally finished the Op. 24 Concerto in the summer, writing the second and third movements with amazing speed once he had at last found his way around the problems posed for so long by the first. This work he dedicated to Schoenberg on the occasion of Schoenberg's sixtieth birthday (13 September 1934). The first of the three songs of Op. 25 was written in July, between the first and second movements of the Concerto, and this opus was completed as well by mid-November. The songs of Opp. 23 and 25 were his first Jone settings.

He still taught composition privately to those pupils who remained, but he could now devote all the rest of his time to his own composition. He wrote the Variations for Piano, Op. 27, in the summer and autumn of 1936, and this was followed by the Op. 28 String Quartet in 1937 and 1938. Both of these are major instrumental works in three movements. Both these works show his continued fascination with symmetry and canon. The Variations for Piano – a structural conundrum that has been interpreted in many ways but certainly is not in the straightforward form that its title would imply – relentlessly explores horizontal symmetry in one of its movements and vertical symmetry in another.

The Variations for Piano was the last of Webern's works to be published by Universal Edition in his lifetime. Emil Hertzka's widow, who had taken over the publishing house at her husband's death, published the work in 1937 and it received its first performance on 26 October of the same year, played by Peter Stadlen in Vienna.

The Quartet, finished after the Anschluß, was another story. In a letter dated 15 December 1937 Webern thanked Elizabeth Sprague Coolidge for her letter of 23 November in which she had offered to commission a work for the Tenth Berkshire Festival (in Massachusetts) in 1938.[3] Her original commission had been for a wind piece, but in the meantime Kolisch had been instrumental in getting this changed to a string quartet, which was what Webern was intending to write next. On 13 April 1938 Webern cabled Mrs Coolidge that the piece was finished and asked her to send the payment by cable in order 'to avoid great loss through later exchange'. In a letter dated 19 April he asks her to pay him in schillings if possible, since if she pays him the $750 she has offered him he will lose one third of it in exchange when it reaches Austria. In a later letter, dated 3 May, he describes his intentions in the piece and characterises it as 'purely lyrical . . . not epic breadth but lyrical conciseness'. It is to be understood as akin not to the three-movement, but to the two-movement sonatas of Beethoven. These two aspects of the Quartet, which Webern felt it so important to impress upon Mrs Coolidge – its lyricism and its debt to Beethoven – have a much more all-encompassing relevance to the understanding of Webern's music than their mention specifically in connection with the Op. 28 Quartet might imply.

The Quartet was published in 1939, by Boosey & Hawkes in London, where Erwin Stein was now the director, having left Universal Edition in Vienna the previous year. Webern's on-going contract with UE had been allowed to lapse by mutual consent. This was the last of his works to be published in his lifetime.

On 1 January 1934 Schoenberg, who was then in New England, wrote Webern a prescient and very touching letter. In it he apologises for not having been in touch at the time of Webern's birthday, nearly a month earlier, and offers belatedly his most fervent wishes for 'whatever good there is for men like us: health, joy in work, creative strength, happiness, and the contentment of one's family and friends' in the terrible place the world had become. He then explains the reason for his silence. For a period of some five or six weeks neither Webern nor Berg, both of whom had 'always spoiled' him with letters, had written to him, and during this time he was 'not only very depressed but completely in despair', as he had, in his isolation in a country that he must have found very foreign, become convinced that both had 'suddenly become Nazis'. He had put the question to Berg ('jokingly', he says, but the real urgency of his question must have been perfectly clear to Berg, who was nothing if not sensitive), and Berg had answered clearly: 'no'. Having had this reassurance he now feels the greatest remorse for ever having had such thoughts about his two dearest friends and in view of Berg's answer he apparently doesn't feel it necessary even to pose the question to Webern. He now regrets 'a thousand times more' that he has ignored Webern's birthday. He goes on to say that for years he has planned to dedicate a 'major work' to Webern on the occasion of his fiftieth birthday but that he now cannot do it because all his recent works have been oriented towards Judaism and would therefore not be appropriate. He ends with the hope that he will 'write a work worthy' of their friendship yet.

Although he had not really been asked the question Webern, like Berg, answered immediately and firmly, in the negative. In his letter of 17 January he claims indeed to feel 'a sense of the most vehement aversion' against his own race because of the antisemitism of so many of its members. Schoenberg was much relieved, but only for a time. The question would continue to haunt him throughout the remainder of his life in exile, and with good reason. In a letter dated 20 June 1937 he finally puts the question to Webern directly. At last Schoenberg has written a work that he feels 'worthy' of dedicating to Webern – his new Violin Concerto, Op. 36 – but before the dedication can be put into print he must ask Webern a question.

I have heard repeatedly in the last few months a rumour which I have not believed and which has been described by various sources, not least by Kolisch, as untrue. Nevertheless, under the circumstances it is necessary that I know the whole truth, and this I can get only through a direct answer to a direct question. Is it true that you have become a supporter, or even a member, of the Nazi party? There are few things that could give me greater joy than your answering no to the questions. But you can see that I could not possibly make a dedication to a supporter of a 'world view' which sees me and others like me as worthless.

I await your answer with the greatest anxiety and accept it as true and hope that you will at least not be insulted by my question: you will know what disappointment people like us have had.

I do not know whether Webern's answer to this letter exists, or, indeed, whether there was one. One supposes that there surely must have been, though it is difficult to imagine what Webern might have said.

According to the American violinist Louis Krasner (of whom we shall hear much more), Schoenberg enquired of him, through Steuermann, whether the rumours of Webern's complicity with the Nazi regime were true. Krasner has said that though he (Krasner) denied them, he believed both Steuermann and Schoenberg knew that he was lying. Schoenberg did in fact dedicate the Violin Concerto to Webern, but, again according to Krasner, he 'toned down' the original wording of the dedication. In June 1947 (after Webern's death) Krasner says that Schoenberg wrote a statement to be included in a new edition of the Webern Concerto (Op. 24) that was being prepared by René Leibowitz. It reads:

Let us – for the moment at least – forget all that might have at one time divided us. For there remains for our future what could only have begun to be realized posthumously: one will have to consider us three – Berg, Webern, Schoenberg – as a unity – a oneness, because we believed in ideals, once perceived, with intensity and selfless devotion; nor would we ever have been deterred from them, even if those who tried might have [may have?] succeeded in confounding us.[4]

But the affair does not seem to be exactly as Krasner has remembered it. I do not know of another piece of correspondence from Schoenberg to Webern between the letter of 20 June 1937 and a postcard dated 11 April 1938, on which Schoenberg writes:

> Dear Toni, how are you? We have not heard from you for such a long time. I only hear something of the terrible state of things. I have heard that you had a string quartet commissioned by Mrs Coolidge. I am very impressed! But do write sometime.

Not a message that suggests either anger or anxiety.

Webern had planned a number of conducting engagements outside Austria in 1934, but all of these except for one with the BBC fell through. He was particularly bitter when a projected performance of *Wozzeck* was withdrawn, for political reasons, from the programme of the ISCM Festival in Florence that year. He had been scheduled to conduct it, and his immediate reaction was to resign his position as president of the Vienna ISCM chapter, an action that was prevented only by the strong-arm techniques of his friend David Josef Bach, who persuaded him that his continued presence was invaluable in opposing the prevailing atmosphere of cultural disintegration.

In the spring of 1935 Webern went once again to England, as in 1934 for a single concert, even on the same date as that of the previous year, 25 April. But on this occasion he conducted three of his own works: his newly finished orchestration of Bach's Ricercar from *The Musical Offering* and two early works, the Op. 1 Passacaglia and the Op. 6 orchestral pieces. In Vienna that year he conducted the Freie Typographia Chorus for the last time on 14 April, his last appearance on Ravag was on 13 July and he conducted a concert of the Vienna chapter of the ISCM on 21 November. The 1935 ISCM Festival took place in Prague in September. Webern was scheduled to conduct the first performance of his Op. 24 Concerto on one of the festival programmes. Still angry about the withdrawal of *Wozzeck* from the Festival the previous year, he decided at the last minute not to attend. Jalowetz conducted the first performance of this work in his place. Luigi Dallapiccola, then aged thirty-one, was in the audience. He wrote in his diary afterwards:

> This evening Heinrich Jalowetz presented the *Concerto Op.* 24 by Anton Webern, a work of incredible conciseness (six minutes of music) and of unique concentration. Every decorative element has been eliminated. Nine instruments take part in the performance: three woodwinds, three brass and two strings with piano.
>
> I could not form a precise idea of the work, too difficult for me to understand; however it seems to represent, without any question, an entire world. We find ourselves before a man who expresses a maximum of ideas with a minimum of words. Although I did not understand the work completely, I had the feeling of finding an aesthetic and stylistic unity as great as I could wish for.
>
> Many people in the hall smiled during the performance; our own delegation also seemed to be in a hilarious mood ('O Latin gaiety, you are not dead yet!' one can read in *Chantecler*. But some laugh at anything).
>
> I have not heard the whole program tonight. Webern compels me to meditate.

In the meantime Webern had composed another piece on a text by Hildegard Jone, an extended work for chorus and orchestra, his Op. 26, *Das Augenlicht*. There were to be no more songs; this work represents a widening of scope and is the first of three large choral works, the other two both called 'cantata', a generic title that has been applied by others to *Das Augenlicht* as well.

In late December of 1935 Webern and Schoenberg, and indeed the world, unexpectedly suffered a very great loss. Early in the morning of Christmas Eve Alban Berg died in the Rudolfspital in Vienna of blood poisoning resulting from an abscess. Although he had suffered with the abscess since August no one had thought of it as life-threatening. Indeed Webern, whose reactions often seem to betray an inability to see beyond the surface of things, announced after visiting him in hospital on 21 December that he had found him much improved.

Berg was only fifty. The shock of his death was very great. Schoenberg, alone and far away in California, wrote to Webern on 15 January, asking for news of Berg's death and expressing his own sorrow. In a poignant acknowledgement of the differences in the public's perception of Berg and its feelings towards himself and Webern he writes of the 'saddest aspect' of Berg's premature death: that, of the three composers, he was the only one who had any success and in whom the public had any faith, and that, had he lived, he would have been able to enjoy these things which his two friends could only long for.

Berg was buried in Hietzing on 28 December. Webern was not at the funeral. As president of the Vienna chapter of the ISCM he had gone to Barcelona for the annual meeting of the selection jury for the festival concerts of the 1936 festival the following April. He was determined to honour his friend's memory by getting Berg's new violin concerto, finished only months before his death, on the programme. He was successful in doing so, and Louis Krasner, who had commissioned the work from Berg, agreed to play the first performance, a year earlier than he had planned. Webern was to conduct. The ISCM Festival must have been a tense one that year, as Germans had been forbidden to take part, a rival German festival having been mounted at Baden-Baden in which only the music of 'pure Aryan' German composers and those foreign composers who had official approval of the Reichsmusikkammer was played.

When Krasner arrived in Vienna at the beginning of April to rehearse the Berg Concerto with Webern he found that Webern had decided he couldn't do it and was not planning to go to Barcelona at all. It was only after an afternoon of strenuous pleading on the part of Krasner, who went to Webern's home and played the concerto for him, that Webern was persuaded to change his mind.[5] He would have been much wiser not to have done so: the whole affair was to be devastating to both his mental health and his reputation, at the same time creating a crisis for the ISCM.

The affair was peculiar from the outset. Krasner relates an odd, almost obsessive, trip to Barcelona in Webern's company. Webern insisted that they travel, together, through Germany – not a direct way of getting from Vienna to Barcelona, and certainly not the route most people took in 1936 – even though Krasner had already purchased a ticket to go the usual route through Switzerland. (Wellesz, Reich and Helene Berg travelled the Swiss route on this occasion.) According to Krasner it transpired that Webern's reason for doing this was to prove to Krasner, a Jew, through first-hand experience, the fallacy of the belief, which was widespread in America and elsewhere, that Jews were in danger in Hitler's Germany. The two men spent the twenty-four-hour overnight train ride talking 'intimately' of politics in a small compartment on a nearly empty international train (a particularly unlikely place for any overt antisemitic activity, according to Krasner). When they reached Munich station Webern insisted on leaving the train and treating Krasner to a beer in the huge station dining hall, which, according to Krasner, was also nearly empty of people. Krasner points out, as Adolph Weiss did also in reminiscences many years later, that for Webern to buy someone else a beer (or indeed to let anyone else buy him one) was quite uncharacteristic, yet on this occasion he insisted. When the train crossed the Swiss border Webern reportedly turned to Krasner and said triumphantly, 'There now, Krasner! Did anyone do anything to you?'

In Barcelona Webern's behaviour continued to be cause for concern. He was allotted three rehearsals to prepare the Berg Concerto. All his conducting life he had been dogged by a meticulousness that had frequently resulted in his having to drop movements from a programme at the last minute because he hadn't had time to get to them in rehearsal. Now this problem took on outrageous proportions. After two of his three rehearsals he had got only a very short distance into the piece (one account says eight bars, Krasner says on one occasion three or four pages, on another six or seven). At the third and last rehearsal Webern was repeatedly asked to run through the entire piece, and after about half an hour he stopped and said that the performance must not take place, 'snatched up his score and rushed from the stage' and locked himself and the score in his hotel room. According to Wellesz, who was also present, it was only after Helene Berg had pleaded with Webern, literally on bended knee, that he relinquished the score so that the performance could go on with another conductor. There ensued a scene that was fairly common in Webern's life as a conductor: the ruins were rescued at the last moment, this time by Hermann Scherchen, who had never seen the Berg score and who prepared the concert in a single half-hour midnight rehearsal borrowed from time he had been allotted to rehearse the concerts he was conducting himself at the festival.

Krasner offers numerous reasons for Webern's spectacular failure at the Barcelona ISCM. He mentions the extreme problems of communication: it is well known that Webern was very soft-spoken and often hard to hear in rehearsal, and that in addition he spoke in a dialect that even Germans could find difficult to understand. He spoke no other languages, and the orchestra in Barcelona, who would have understood French, did not understand even High German. This problem was always overcome in Webern's London performances by having an interpreter present. Then Krasner blames the Casals orchestra, which he says had no experience with modern music (thus implying that they probably couldn't play it). He does not explain how it was that this same orchestra managed after all to perform the Berg Concerto, as well as all the other contemporary music of the ISCM festival with other conductors. Nor does he seem to be aware of the fact that Webern had conducted this orchestra before, successfully, in his own music and that of Schoenberg, in 1932. But Krasner's final reason, the one he considers the most important, is that Webern simply didn't have the necessary technique as a conductor. He says:

> But the worst problem of all was Webern's rehearsal technique, if it could be called that.

> For poor Webern, ... Barcelona was a humiliating defeat. The situation was beyond that; he didn't have the technique.

How can one explain then the successful concerts Webern had conducted in Vienna? The orchestra he worked with was not a wholly professional one. Most of the players were conservatory people, or amateurs, or those who loved Webern. And they worked endlessly. ... Only when they were ready did they play. So he really coached them. He didn't conduct so much as coach.

It is perhaps at this point that one begins to suspect that Krasner harboured some sort of resentment against Webern, perhaps because Webern refused to see the reality of Hitler's antisemitism, perhaps for some other reason. Because in fact Webern had had considerable experience conducting professional orchestras: the Berlin Philharmonic (in June 1923), the orchestras of the Munich Tonhalle, Frankfurt Radio and Berlin Radio (in November 1929), the BBC Symphony in London, where he was welcomed year after year; and in Vienna the orchestras of the Konzertverein and the State Opera, the Vienna Philharmonic and the Vienna Symphony Orchestra. None of these was an amateur group, all operated to set schedules and Webern had had notable successes with all of them over the course of thirteen years.

It would seem to me that the most likely explanation of Webern's débâcle in Barcelona in 1936 is one he suggested himself in a letter to his friend David Josef Bach in which he described the incident.

> no one considered at all, but really not at all, that the première of Berg's last work – in memoriam – was at stake. It was an *immeasurable torment*. A hell. I can take the responsibility for what I have done. The contrary [carrying on with a performance that he considered under-rehearsed and imperfect], however, would not have been possible. (HM: 457)

Webern had very recently lost a much-loved friend whom he had known from his youth (three months is a very short time in terms of grief) and he had now the responsibility of bringing that friend's last and very great work to life for the first time with only three rehearsals. It was too much to ask.

Webern was so devastated and broken that he could think only of getting back home, in spite of the fact that another performance of the Berg Concerto with Krasner was scheduled less than two weeks later in London and his plan had been to travel straight there from Spain. He fled to Mödling the day after the performance. When he appeared in London on 29 April he had recovered his composure sufficiently to conduct what he had no way of knowing would be his last two performances for the BBC. The performance of the Berg Concerto and two movements of the *Lyric Suite* on 1 May was a great success, as was that of Bruckner's Seventh Symphony two nights later.

In fact this Bruckner Seventh with the BBC Symphony was Webern's last appearance anywhere as a conductor. He was only fifty-two, and in a normal world his career would have continued for decades, but in Austria in the 1930s and 40s this was not to be. Neither his association with Schoenberg nor his style of composition was to be tolerated. Now, with the fascist government that had taken over in 1934, his association with David Josef Bach and the cultural organisations of the Social Democratic Party also worked against him. He was finished. One may even be able to understand a little his hope that a National Socialist regime (*any* new regime, particularly one that called itself 'Socialist') might be an improvement on the status quo.

There is no question that Webern had certain difficulties as a conductor. His insistence on perfection (in others as in himself) meant that he frequently spent so much time on the details of one work in rehearsal that he had to cancel another because he had not had time to get round to rehearsing it. He always conducted from the score; Maria Halbich says that he considered conducting from memory simply a display of virtuosity for virtuosity's sake. Gordon Claycombe, one of his American students, has written of his style of conducting: 'Webern was no baton virtuoso – he was ungainly on the podium – with his head buried in the score and his arms flailing the air above.' He says, however, that Steuermann (like Berg) considered Webern to be 'one of the truly great conductors of our time'. Claycombe continues: 'I don't believe enough has been said or written about Webern's outstanding interpretations of Beethoven, Bruckner, and especially, Mahler. But the intensity, freshness, novelty and sensitiveness of his interpretations was an experience one could never forget'.[6] The rare recordings that exist today of his conducting bear witness to this. To my knowledge the only recordings that survive of Webern conducting are one from 1932 of his arrangement of the Schubert German Dances and the BBC recording of the Berg Violin Concerto made in 1936.[7] In both cases every note has been placed with extreme care. His was an intense and introspective style of conducting, exaggerated in its expressiveness and absolutely meticulous. Who can know where it would have led him in normal times? He might have been too pains-taking ever to have achieved the pinnacle, but he almost certainly would have produced many very memorable performances.

The exodus of friends and associates accelerated considerably after the Anschluß. Webern's long-time student Kurt Manschinger (Manschinger had been his first student when he moved to Mödling in 1918) and his old and dear friends Heinrich Jalowetz and his wife escaped to Prague in 1938 and from there to America. In the same year David Josef Bach moved to Switzerland, as did two more of his students, Willi Reich and Siegfried Oehlgiesser. Also in 1938 fellow Schoenberg students and colleagues from Society for Private Musical Performances days, Egon Wellesz and Erwin Stein; the violinists Oskar Adler, a contemporary of Schoenberg, and Arnold Rosé, who had been much revered in Vienna and a staunch champion of music of the Schoenberg circle for many years; and Webern's student Emil Spira all emigrated to England. Mark Brunswick, Rudolph Réti, Krenek and Zemlinsky fled to the US in 1938, as did Stefan Wolpe and Schoenberg's son-in-law and former student Felix Greissle. Rudolph Kurzmann, in whose home Webern had given his annual lecture series, also departed for America, though his wife Rita, a pianist, remained in Vienna, emigrating to South America after the war. Very few of Webern's old associates remained. Even his beloved cousin Ernst Diez emigrated to the US. His old friend Josef Polnauer and Schoenberg's son Georg, both Jews, went into hiding for many years,

11 Webern and his friend Ludwig Zenk, 1937.

though Webern continued to see both on occasion. Two other close friends, his old student (and his most promising, according to Webern) Ludwig Zenk and his singer friend Josef Hueber, became Nazis. Both Hueber and Hans Humpelstetter, another friend from the Mödling Men's Chorus, joined the army (Zenk was refused for health reasons). At last Webern's life had been split asunder, divided into those who could not tolerate the madness of the National Socialists and those who enthusiastically embraced it. The overwhelming majority belonged to the former group. Unfortunately Webern himself did not.

8 1938–45 After the Anschluß

Who speaks of victory? To endure is everything.

Rilke, from 'Requiem for Wolf Graf von Kalckreuth':
the final entry in Webern's last notebook

At four o'clock in the afternoon on 12 March 1938 Hitler's troops marched into Austria and the Catholic government of Kurt von Schuschnigg capitulated. According to Louis Krasner he and Webern were in Webern's house in Mödling (Maria Enzersdorf) talking about the Schoenberg violin concerto, which had not yet had its first performance. Krasner later described the scene:

> We were talking, getting along fine, when suddenly, clutching my arm, he asked, 'What time is it?' I looked: just 4 o'clock. He rushed to the radio and turned it on. Then we heard the voice of Schuschnigg saying, 'German troops have just crossed the Austrian frontier, and I have told the Austrian soldiers to withdraw in order to avoid brother fighting brother.'
>
> Webern caught hold of me, and exclaimed, 'Krasner, here's your coat – run – go home!' ... 'Go quickly!' Webern said. 'Down two streets in the back – find a taxi!'[1]

Krasner tries to make a point about Webern's personal involvement with the National Socialists from this scene, on the evidence that Webern clearly had privileged information about what was going to happen that afternoon and when it was going to happen. I think that in this case, as in his recounting of the Barcelona débâcle quoted in chapter 7, Krasner is not to be considered an altogether reliable – or at the least not an objective – witness. It is well known that Webern's son Peter, who lived in Webern's house, had been a member of the Nazi party for some time, so it surely would have been surprising if Webern had not known the particulars of the Anschluß before the event. Privileged information, yes, but not proof that Webern was himself a Nazi in collusion with the invading forces. What the incident does seem to make clear is that Webern no longer held the illusions concerning the National Socialists' treatment of Jews that he had had two years earlier when he and Krasner had travelled to Barcelona together. (One is saddened when reading elsewhere that Webern almost immediately removed Humplik's bust of Mahler from its position in the livingroom, where it could be seen from the street, to the bedroom, where it could not.)

Krasner's whole account is coloured by the existence of a letter written to the Humpliks on the same day, in which Webern says 'I am completely absorbed in my work and cannot be disturbed'. He was writing the Op. 28 String Quartet, not only at this time, but, clearly, on this very day. If Krasner did visit him on this particular afternoon (and the letter throws even this fact into some doubt) it must not have been a welcome interruption; small wonder that Webern packed him off unceremoniously at the first opportunity.

The events of that afternoon and their inevitable and immediate aftermath brought even further ruin to a life that was already noteworthy for its decline. Soon after the Anschluß an exhibition of 'degenerate art' was mounted at the Künstlerhaus in Vienna, modelled after one that had occurred in Munich a year earlier. Webern's music was included. It now became clear that, though he was not himself Jewish, he had been sufficiently tainted by his association with Schoenberg to make his music unacceptable to the ruling government. Very soon Universal Edition was taken over by the Nazis, and both publication and performance of his music were banned. The Austrian chapter of the ISCM, of which Webern was president, was disbanded in 1938 – an Austrian chapter had become a paralogism when Austria ceased to exist – thus he was unable to travel to England for the first performance of his new work, *Das Augenlicht*, at the ISCM Festival in London on 17 June 1938.

When England and France declared war on 3 September 1939 Webern's remaining nominal ties with Ravag ended. Nearly all of his students had fled by this time. Universal Edition, who had once published and enthusiastically supported his music, now offered him small occasional jobs as reader, proofreader and arranger. Webern's financial situation became desperate. In Nb4, where his monthly accounts from the years 1924 to 1945 are carefully recorded, income is entered in two columns: his own regular monthly income appears in the lefthand column, the monthly contributions of his three working children, gifts and special one-time-only payments on the right. The righthand column for March 1939 records Webern's last payment from UE as a composer. His total income in 1940, including his children's regular monthly contributions (which amounted to RM100 most months) and a gift of RM1000 from Werner Reinhardt, was RM3857.98. In 1940 the Reichsmark was worth about one-tenth of a pound sterling, the equivalent of approximately £1.60 in today's terms. Webern's own income was only RM55 in February, March, May and June and RM52.43 in July; he recorded no income at all in August. There are no accounts after February 1945.

Webern's political position has always remained somewhat vague; while there is sufficient documentary as well as anecdotal evidence to provide an unsettling picture of a man who without question believed in Hitler's Third Reich – and for an amazingly long time – no one has ever provided incontrovertible evidence of his actually having been a member of the Nazi Party, as Schoenberg is alleged to have declared in a letter that no one has ever been able to produce.[2] Wildgans admitted of no political sympathies whatever:

> He did not warm towards antisemitism. . . . It was therefore natural that Webern found nothing positive in the philosophy of national

socialism or in the whole complex of fascism, and as a result isolated himself from both national socialism and the world it encompassed ... the ineluctable drive of national socialism towards war kept Webern, a convinced pacifist, as far away as possible from the Nazi ideology.[3]

There are various difficulties with this argument, of course, the most obvious being that antisemitism did not represent the whole of Nazi ideology, though it is surely remembered as the most horrific act of a regime that was insupportable in every other way as well. And convinced pacifist Webern may have been, but this is certainly an arguable point in view of letters written to his friend Josef Hueber in the early 1940s, in which he demonstrated an almost manic enthusiasm for Germany's military conquests. On 2 May 1940 he wrote to Hueber, who was serving in the army:

> And does it not all go on apace? (This most recent outcome! Magnificent![4]) But not only the outward process! The inner as well! It is uplifting.

At Christmas of 1941:

> I feel the Japanese entry into the war as a *fundamental, decisive turning point*. As a mighty event![5] ... who knows yet what will come from this nation! I must say, these thoughts fill me with quite special confidence.
>
> Because, as I imagine it, they appear to me – the Japanese people – as a *completely healthy race*! Through and through! Will the new strength not draw us upward? ... I see it *only so*! I cannot see it otherwise! And I am happy about it!!! I would like to say still more about this.

And later, on 25 February 1942, 'What did I say about the Japanese? Is it not so now?'[6]

Webern's association with David Josef Bach and his direction of Bach's two proletarian institutions – the Workers' Symphony Concerts and the Vienna Choral Society – in the 1920s and early 1930s as well as his association with the Freie Typographia add confusing threads to the fabric. Bach was not only an employer but a close friend; he was also strongly placed in the socialist government which was in power in Vienna up to 1934. It was presumably on the strength of these activities that Humphrey Searle, a Webern student during this period, wrote of Webern as 'a convinced social democrat' who was opposed to the fascist government of Schuschnigg and 'believed that he might fare better under the Nazis, who at least called themselves socialists'. Searle labelled Webern an 'idealist',[7] a word that implies more political involvement than Wildgans' 'pacifist'; clearly the involvement suggested is with the left. There is ample evidence however that Webern himself wished to avoid an explicit association with the socialists. In April of 1929, after considerable success conducting for Ravag, he had declined consideration for an executive position in the broadcasting system. In explaining his decision to Schoenberg he wrote that he did not want the position because of its political implications: he would be working as a trustee of the Social Democratic Party. The fact is that Webern seems to have led a schizophrenic sort of existence during the 1920s and early 1930s: at home, as his children reached adulthood three of the four became Nazis, as were, later, two of his sons-in-law (his son, Peter, and his youngest daughter, Christine, and her husband were particularly zealous), while his professional life in the city was led almost entirely in the company of, and was financed almost entirely by, socialists and Jews.

Recently Fred Prieberg has tried to demonstrate that Webern was a Nazi on the ground that he applied for and received money from the Reichsmusikkammer (the Third Reich's Ministry of Music).[8] The fact is that Webern, in 1940, when he had several children and grandchildren living under his roof or nearby and, as we have seen, was practically destitute as the result of having had all his former sources of income cut off, made an application to the Reichsmusikkammer, which was administered by Goebbels, for an artist's grant (a Künstlerdank) and was given one. In Prieberg's eyes this was a damning action. Another observer might see it as the desperate attempt of a father and grandfather to keep his family from starving. The

Reichsmusikkammer was the official government agency, and applying to the government for a grant if one is eligible for it is the natural avenue of any citizen who is in need. While starving oneself for a principle may be seen as admirable, forcing such a fate unnecessarily on one's family is surely less so. One can also imagine that Webern may have felt that, since the Reichsmusikkammer and its associated government agencies had been responsible for the cessation of his income as a conductor and a composer, there was a certain moral justification in accepting money from this source if it was forthcoming.

Prieberg finds every aspect of Webern's conduct with respect to the Künstlerdank reprehensible. According to his account, which he bases on documents from the Third Reich currently held in Berlin, Webern first invited a search of his political activities and connections and received a clean bill of health. Perhaps 'allowed' would be more accurate than 'invited', as this was a process that anyone would certainly have known to be the first requirement of such an application to any agency of the fanatical Third Reich. Prieberg quotes the local department's submission to Goebbels, recommending Webern for a grant on the grounds that his personal political loyalty and conviction overrode the fact that his music was 'subjectively and intellectually close to the style of the Schoenberg circle!'; of the several factors that contributed to the clear certificate granted him nearly all had to do with the active participation of his children and their spouses in various organs of National Socialism. His son Peter had been a National Socialist when the party was forbidden in Austria and membership in it therefore illegal, and his daughter Christine was a member of the Bund deutscher Mädchen, the female branch of the Hitler Youth. Webern's own most incriminating activity seems to have been that he regularly read the National Socialist press, an exercise that might be seen as rather less than damning in a society where this party was a great power. Prieberg also finds Webern's solicitation of a letter of support from a musicologist who was in a strong position with the Reichsmusikkammer a subject for scorn, though one might easily argue that this also represents a sensible course of action for anyone who had decided to make such an application. And, finally, Prieberg claims that the grant given Webern (RM250, then worth about £25, or about £400 in today's terms) was larger than the amount usually awarded, and this he sees as a reward for Webern's complicity with the Nazi regime.

The sums recorded by Webern in his accounts book show that he received artist grants from the Reichsmusikkammer (identified as Künstlerdank) in the amounts of RM250 (and perhaps an additional RM50 as well – these two figures are written separately, but both in red pencil and enclosed in the same red pencilled box) in March 1941; RM40 in December 1941 and RM50 in December in each of the years 1942–4 (by 1944 RM50 was worth about £19 in today's terms); and from the city of Vienna (Künstlerhilfe Wien) in the amount of RM200 twice, in February and again in October of 1942.

In any case the fact of Webern's membership or non-membership in the Nazi Party seems to me to be of little consequence. What cannot be ignored or glossed over is his obvious and overwhelming enthusiasm for the pan-German Reich and for Hitler, its architect, whether he was a card-carrying member of the latter's corrupt club or not. He was not a new convert to the idea of German superiority: intense pan-German chauvinism had been an important element in his makeup from the beginning. Many of his friends have commented on his strong German nationalism, and we have seen examples of this as early as 1902, when he described the character of Hans Sachs not as a good man, but as a good *German* man (see p. 30), and three years later when Dürer's self-portrait impressed him as 'the most wonderful image', not of man, but of *German* man (see p. 42). His perception of German culture as the only one worth considering and of German morality and discipline as the only salvation in a world that he perceived to have gone badly wrong were attitudes that were an inextricable part of his nature – and understandable, I think, when one considers the German tradition in thinking and the arts (a few days in Vienna give one some understanding of the famous Viennese insularity: with forebears like Haydn, Mozart, Beethoven, Schubert, Brahms, Mahler, plus the German neighbours Bach, Goethe *et al.*, one might be very tempted to look no further) and the political and cultural chaos that was rampant in Vienna and Germany in the 1920s and early 1930s.

Ironically, in view of the particular direction German nationalism was to take under Hitler, Webern's convictions about German superiority were shared by Schoenberg, who was so pleased to have discovered in the early 1920s a technique of composition that would ensure the superiority of *German* music for the next hundred years (or for centuries, according to whose report of this memorable occasion one believes). Stuckenschmidt has said that both Webern and Schoenberg were monarchists.[9] Berg wrote to his wife on 11 September 1919:

> Schoenberg, by the way, has quite gone off the Social Democrats, but doesn't really know what political line to take. His idea is, go back to the old régime as quickly as possible, but do things better – almost a monarchist position, in fact. (Berg: 246)

Schoenberg said as much himself, in an essay entitled 'My Attitude Toward Politics' written in 1950:

> When the First World War began, ... I became a monarchist. Also at this time and after the unfortunate ending of the war and for many years thereafter, I considered myself as a monarchist.[10]

And Krasner has quoted Webern as saying, when asked during the famous trip to Barcelona how he could follow the Nazis' 'political and social thoughts' when all of his best friends were Jews, 'Even Schoenberg, had he not been a Jew, would have been quite different!' This remark, in the wording given it by Krasner, is surely either one of history's most inanely obvious observations or ambiguous to the point of being meaningless. But, judging from the context, what Krasner presumably understood Webern to have said was that Schoenberg was such a strong German nationalist that, had his racial origins not made such a position impossible for him, he himself would have supported the Nazi regime.

In letters written to Josef Hueber in the early 1940s, some of which have already been quoted above, Webern shows great enthusiasm for Hitler and Nazi domination as the German world's ordained and proper destiny. Moldenhauer quotes a particularly damning letter that I have not seen, written on 4 March 1940, after having read *Mein Kampf*, which was given him by Hueber:

> The book has brought me much enlightenment. . . . What I believe I see at present makes me supremely confident! I see it coming, the pacification of the entire world. At first east of the Rhine as far as— yes, how far? This will depend on the USA. But probably as far as the Pacific Ocean! Yes, I believe this, I do believe, and I cannot see it any other way! (HM: 526–7)

Maria Halbich, the only one of Webern's children to resist the pull towards National Socialism, has said that her mother was always wary of the Nazi Party and warned Webern especially about Hitler, whom she saw as a great danger from the beginning. Her warnings seem however to have fallen on deaf ears. On 2 May 1940, immediately following Germany's occupation of Denmark and Norway, Webern writes:

> though this is called unification, it also absolutely indicates a process of inner *purification*. That is Germany today! But only under *National socialism*!!! No other way! This is the *new* state, for which the country has been preparing for over twenty years! Yet it is *a new country*, as it has never existed before! It is a *new creation*! A creation of this singular man!!! You see, you sense my concern: one might (in the end) accept as commonplace what could occur *only once*, what is possible only through precisely this nature, this *unique* creator.

He returns to the subject of this predestined state, and to its symbol, the swastika, in a letter written on 21 December 1940. (During this year the Netherlands, Belgium and France had all fallen to Germany; Italy had declared war on France and Great Britain and invaded and occupied much of north Africa; Germany had wreaked terrible havoc on Britain through its air attacks; Germany, Italy and Japan had concluded a pact in Berlin in September; Romania and Hungary had joined the Axis alliance; and Roosevelt's aid to Britain had been denounced by Germany as 'moral aggression'.)

> I have made very important and interesting discoveries in *Stefan George*: in 'Stern des Bundes', in which he gives a *doctrine*, the many facets of which have been realised today – but already in 1914!!! and in the *'New Reich'* (1921), in which the foundation of things is directly named: he speaks of the *'true symbol'* on the 'national banner'!!!

Webern also writes with great fervour about the prophetic nature of these two works of Stefan George in letters to Humpelstetter dated Christmas 1940 and 20 February 1941.

On 22 June 1941 Germany invaded Russia. On 13 July Russia concluded a mutual aid treaty with Britain. In a letter to Hueber written on 18 July Webern alluded to these events.

> One can scarcely understand anymore what is happening! . . .—Have you read the statements of the men in the Kremlin? These plans are fiendish, but fundamentally so *dilettantish*, so ridiculous! And again *Providence* strikes, I mean this in the most literal sense (who has really known, accurately 'foreseen'?) , the *'arms from the hand'* of the enemy (again in a literal sense). And so it will all go on! ((*Continue*)) It is stupendous!

It is difficult for a non-German today to believe the degree of naïveté – not to say blindness – shown in these letters. Yet it does seem to be of a piece with the unbridled enthusiasms and the extremes of contempt that we have seen to be characteristic of Webern since the days of his youth. No one could accuse Webern of antisemitism: he is known to have hidden and helped a number of Jewish friends and acquaintances in the dark days after the Anschluß, among them Josef Polnauer (who as an albino[11] was more or less free to roam the streets of Vienna without attracting special attention and was a regular visitor to the house at Maria Enzersdorf) and Georg Schoenberg, the composer's son, who remained in Vienna throughout the war. Both were offered refuge in the house at Maria Enzersdorf on occasion, and

Schoenberg occupied the Weberns' apartment there after the Weberns themselves had fled to Mittersill, a village in the mountains near Salzburg, for safety. (According to our old friend Krasner, Schoenberg was nearly arrested by the Russian occupation forces at the close of the war as a result of Webern's protection. Krasner says that the cellar belonging to the Webern apartment was found to be filled with arms and Nazi propaganda, and that, ironically, as the person occupying the flat, the refugee Schoenberg was assumed to be the owner of these things. This story has not been related by anyone else.)

Yet one is tempted to wonder if Webern might not in fact have accepted the whole Nazi package if the conditions of his life had been different. The zealous German nationalism that persisted throughout his life and led him ultimately to place his hopes in Hitler, in combination with his youthful irritations with what struck him as the pretentious precocity and personal unpleasantness of 'Jewish boys' and 'Jewish girls', make it apparent that he was not particularly sympathetic to Jews at the beginning of his life in Vienna. But, as Fate would have it, in the end most of his closest friends and associates were Jewish, so particular affection seems to have prevented, or superseded, what might otherwise have become general censure. His was a complex situation, and though his ideas on German nationalism leave no room for doubt, his great enthusiasm for Hitler and his conquests is less straightforward. Webern was the head of a family who could not leave Austria. Who can say to what extent his actions were determined by the practicalities of keeping this family alive and to what extent by a real belief in Hitler as the saviour of European civilisation? From the beginning he seems to have been – perhaps he was forced to be by his situation – an opportunist in the most literal sense of the word. He did whatever work he was allowed to do for whoever was in power, be they socialist or fascist, but he avoided being drawn into either camp in a political way. (To my knowledge his enthusiastic ravings about the events of the war were restricted to letters to his friend Hueber, who undoubtedly shared these views.) The government – the 'singular man' – he so trusted to restore the old Germany was also hell-bent on systematically destroying a large portion of its population: the one aim could not be divorced from the other. This Webern seems never to have understood. In this situation to be silent was tantamount to collusion; in these horrific times naïveté was a great misfortune. I have drawn the comparison between Webern and Bruckner before;[12] one wonders how this other intensely naïve genius would have behaved in 1940.

Certainly Webern's loyalties and presumed loyalties caused considerable consternation within the circle of old friends and associates. Eduard Steuermann, who reportedly was often angered by Webern's naïve assertions that everything was certain to turn out all right in the end, left Vienna in 1936 and appears finally to have broken with Webern some two years later. A letter to Webern dated 12 August 1938 is friendly, but nearly a year later Webern asks anxiously why Steuermann has not answered his recent letters, complaining – curiously – of not having had a letter since 24 December 1937. David Lewin writes:

> I remember very clearly Steuermann's reaction when he learned of Webern's death. The phone rang in the middle of my piano lesson – I would have been 12 years old, I believe – and when he came back, he said that we would have to discontinue the lesson, as he was too upset to continue. I asked him what was wrong, and he said that someone who had once been a close friend had died. At the time, I had no idea who Webern was – the Leibowitz book, from which I learned about W., had not appeared yet in the US, and Steuermann never mentioned Webern. . . . [Steuermann] didn't play Op. 27, which W. had dedicated to him as a peace offering, until long after Webern's death and the end of the war.[13]

Webern's correspondence with Kolisch continued until 1939, then ceased, presumably for the same reasons as that with Steuermann had earlier. Both men had had first-hand knowledge of Webern's enthusiasm for the Third Reich.

Schoenberg's anxiety concerning Webern's relationship with the

Nazis was examined in chapter 7. Although letters became less frequent as time went by, Schoenberg's correspondence with Webern did not stop until the terrible days towards the end of the war when letters could not get through. A long and friendly letter dated 8 July 1939 is devoted largely to an account of Schoenberg's progress with his book *Fundamentals of Musical Composition*, after which he asks Webern not to think him 'an old woman' because of his long and detailed description of himself and his own concerns. Later he tells Webern that he is growing old, and has had to give up smoking and drinking, though happily this has made him feel so well that he has been able to take up tennis again. He writes about his wife and young children and congratulates Webern on his new grandchild (Christine's first child, Karin, born on 3 October 1938); he writes with nostalgia and sadness of old friends – Polnauer, Bach, Jalowetz. And he mentions Webern's work on his Cantata (the first), making it clear that Webern has written to him in the meantime. Like the postcard of the previous year, this is a friendly letter, completely free of tensions.

Only two further Schoenberg–Webern letters survive, from 28 December 1940 and 28 January 1941. In the first Schoenberg reveals that the arrival of another Schoenberg child is imminent and writes of the great joy he derives from the two young children already in his household. He also tells Webern about a recent Columbia recording of *Pierrot Lunaire* that has pleased him greatly. He asks Webern if he thinks it is possible that Schoenberg could send him a set of the recordings, but then answers his own question: 'Sadly, I must doubt it'. The letter closes with the usual warm greetings.

The last surviving communication is not so much a letter as an announcement:

Dear friend: briefly,

my wife gave birth to a son yesterday,
on 27 January at 10.00 p.m.
My wife and the child are in good health.
We have not yet decided upon a name.[14]

Most heartfelt greetings
[signed:] Your Arnold Schoenberg

Though Webern had not been able to travel to London for the occasion of the first performance of *Das Augenlicht*, one of his admirers did make the trip. The young Luigi Dallapiccola, who had been so impressed with Webern's Op. 24 Concerto at Prague three years earlier, heard the performance. In his diary he wrote a long account of the piece and his impressions of it.

> Webern's music is too new to reveal at sight-reading all its qualities of tone-colour. The wish, in fact, to approach the work of a Master with whom I was not familiar enough, was one of the main reasons for my trip. To hear *Das Augenlicht* it was worth going all the way through green France and crossing the Channel, amidst a revel of sea-gulls.
> . . .
> Anton Webern is a lonely flower who does not resemble any one. He is completely different from Arnold Schönberg, who was his teacher; completely different from Alban Berg, his brotherly friend. .
> . . .
> What struck me mainly in *Das Augenlicht*, at a first and – alas – single audition, was the quality of sound.
> . . .
> Webern proves to us, even when he does not work in a strictly contrapuntal direction, that two notes by the celesta, a light touch of the glockenspiel, a barely audible tremolo in the mandolin, are able to bridge abysses which, at first sight, seem to be separated by incalculable distances.
> . . .
> *Das Augenlicht*, on first hearing, reveals itself to be poetic and harmonious. The voice and the instruments, often at great distance, seem to oppose each other's sonorous plans. The orchestral score seems to be enriched by mysterious vibrations as though performed under a glass-bowl. The musical construction has an inner rhythm, which has nothing in common with the mechanical rhythm. . . . The

sound, for the time being, is the most powerful emotional impression I received from this work. A sound, by itself, which makes me consider *Das Augenlicht* as one of the fundamental works of our time.

. . .

After finishing the String Quartet Webern began immediately on his next work, a cantata of three movements for soprano soloist, chorus and orchestra, on poems of Hildegard Jone. This he wrote between the summer of 1938 and the end of 1939. He gave the first full-score manuscript of the central movement, 'Kleiner Flügel Ahornsamen', to the Humpliks for Christmas in 1939. In the accompanying letter he says he is sure that they will understand everything 'from the "drawing" that has appeared through the notes'. And indeed it is almost an example of 'eye music', in which the voice line, singing of maple keys fluttering to the ground to sink there and ascend again as trees, is surrounded by two- and three-note fragments in first one instrument then another, like seeds at the mercy of the wind. From Webern's letters to the Humpliks one supposes that they did not read music, but his faith in what they could tell from his scores was never daunted by this fact.

Webern completed two more works after the Op. 29 Cantata and left sketches for another. The Variations for Orchestra, Op. 30, his only twelve-note piece for large orchestra, was written between April and November of 1940. There is correspondence with both Stein in London and Reich in Switzerland in which Webern tries to interest someone in either publishing or performing this work. Eventually it was given a performance, in Winterthur on 3 March 1943, with Hermann Scherchen conducting, but it was not published in Webern's lifetime. Webern travelled to Switzerland for the performance in what would be both his last trip abroad and the last time he was to hear his own music performed. He stayed in the home of the Swiss patron Werner Reinhardt, where he enjoyed fabulous delicacies (coffee, cigars) that were no longer available in Austria. He wrote a long letter to Hueber, describing the trip. One of the things he mentions is the attentiveness of the German consul in Zurich, who seems to have been keeping him under rather close surveillance.

> I must confess that I was overjoyed – never before had it happened to me that a representative of my fatherland had paid any attention to me! Now just consider my present situation here at home! May the homeland be kind towards me only outside its borders? But I see it as a good omen and as a reward for my loyalty. (HM: 551)

Many have found his references in this letter to 'my fatherland' and 'the homeland' difficult to accept with equanimity. They are difficult to reconcile with remarks he had made upon leaving Austria and entering Germany during the course of his first conducting tour in 1929 (cf. p. 134).

The only work composed in the years 1941–3 is the Second Cantata, Op. 31; this was to be Webern's last cantata – as well as his last work – though there are fairly extensive sketches for a third cantata, which began life as a concerto, in his last sketchbook. The Op. 31 Cantata is a large work, consisting of six movements, all on Jone texts, for soprano and bass soloists, mixed chorus and orchestra. The texts of about half the movements are overtly religious. In a letter to Hildegard Jone written shortly after completing it, Webern outlined ways in which he perceived his work to fulfil the requirements of a *Missa brevis*. This perception influenced his decision concerning the final order of movements. There is no reason however to suppose that this interpretation had occurred to him while he was writing the piece.

Webern's family life continued apace during these years of terrible stress, though the diary entries are very few in number and terse. His household must have been a busy and crowded one, with four grown children, one son-in-law and later a second, and a growing number of children in a rather fluid state of residence. On 2 June 1938, three months before the Anschluß, his youngest daughter Christine, who was five months pregnant, married a zealous Nazi storm trooper,

12 Postcard to Webern from Hildegard Jone dated Advent 1941: line drawing self-portrait with opening text of third movement of Webern's Cantata No. 2, Op. 31.

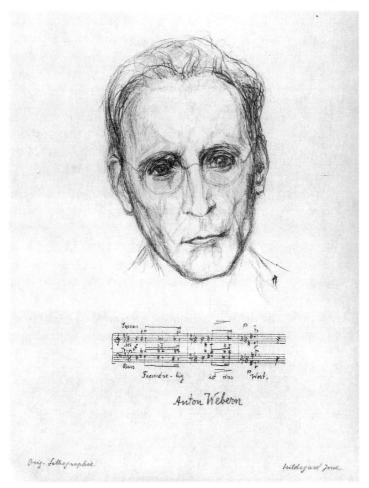

13 Line drawing of Webern done by Hildegard Jone in 1943, with opening bars of fifth movement of Webern's Cantata No. 2, Op. 31.

Benno Mattel, in a civil ceremony in Mödling. The only entry from 1938 in Nb6 records the birth of the couple's daughter Karin on 3 October. The next entry, on the same page, sadly records the stillbirth of Amalie's second child on 27 March 1939. The birth of Christine's second child, Ute, on 19 June 1940 is recorded on page 54 of Sketchbook V, on the seventh page of sketches for the Op. 30

Variations for Orchestra. The activities of Webern's son Peter run throughout the notebook and the late sketchbooks: he trained in the work corps, was drafted into the military on 16 September 1940, then released because of heart trouble on 19 November of the same year only to be called back into service on 24 February 1942; in the meantime he had married on 5 April 1941. On page 111 of Sketchbook V, amidst sketches for what would eventually become the last movement of the Op. 31 Cantata, 'Gelockert aus die Schoße' (not at the top of these sketches, as various authors have stated), the birth of Christine's third daughter (Liesa) on 17 November 1942 is noted. On the second page of the final sketchbook, where Op. 31 is still being sketched, Maria's wedding on 20 May 1943 is recorded, and on page 35 of this book the birth of her son, Peter, on 9 February 1944. The comings and goings of the elder Peter continue to cover the margins of the sketchbook. The final diary records appear in the last sketchbook, in the bottom left-hand corner of page 37, and tell of the flight of Maria and Christine with their children to Mittersill on 7 June 1944 and of the elder Weberns' visit with them there from 25 July to 16 August of the same year. No further family events were recorded – or, if they were, the records no longer exist – though they are revealed in letters. In a letter dated 7 November 1944 Webern tells Hans Humpelstetter of the birth of Amalie's son Christian on 13 September: 'A sixth grandchild has come to us: my eldest daughter . . . has had a baby.' And a final, devastating, family event fills a letter to the Humpliks dated 8 March 1945, which begins 'The thing I have to tell you! Our Peter lives no more; he departed this life on February 14.' (Peter had visited his wife at their home in Perchtoldsdorf on 10 February and his parents the following day. That evening he had boarded a train for a long slow journey back to active duty in Yugoslavia. His train was blown up by low-flying bombers three days later. His wife – and, from her, his parents – received news of his death only on 3 March.)

In 1944 and 1945 Webern's letters to Humpelstetter and the Humpliks were increasingly concerned with bombings and destruction, shortages and the breakdown of local communications and

14 Peter Webern, 1943.

transportation. On 29 April 1944 he announced to the Humpliks that he had been called up in the air-raid protection police (he was sixty) and was living in a barrack, away from family and work, where his day consisted of 'carrying sand and so on' from 6 a.m. to 5 p.m. In the autumn of that year Josef Humplik's studio in Vienna's nineteenth district was hit by bombs on three occasions, and was finally completely destroyed. In a letter dated 26 February 1945, in which he clearly had not yet heard of his son's death, Webern told Humpelstetter that trains between Mödling and Vienna had not been running

15 Mittersill in 1989 (photograph by Sharland).

for eight days, and that water, electricity and gas were in short supply. (This was the last letter to reach Humpelstetter before he was taken prisoner of war.) Finally, on 31 March, Webern and his wife and their eldest daughter, Amalie, and her two children (the younger only six months old) set out on foot to make their way to Mittersill, in the mountains in the Pinzgau, towards Salzburg, where they joined Christine and Maria and their children in what was hoped would be a safe haven. Six days after the flight to Mittersill, on 5 April, Mödling fell to the Russians. The house and its belongings at 8 Im Auholz were largely laid waste by the occupying soldiers who used it as a barrack.

In Mittersill the entire Webern family lived for a time in the home of the Halbichs, Maria's parents-in-law, at Burk 31. Amalie Waller wrote later of the '17 persons pressed together in the smallest possible space' (*DAW*: 112). All three of Webern's sons-in-law were in the army: Benno Mattel was in Mittersill; Gunter Waller, who had served earlier in the war and sustained an injury that had resulted in his release from active service, had been seconded at the end of March into the Volkssturm, a hastily formed troop of under- and over-age men who were sent to Trieste; and Fred Halbich was a prisoner of war in Yugoslavia, where he was to remain until 1948. There were six young children in the household, and there was considerable antagonism between Frau Halbich and Frau Webern. Life in the house at Burk 31 must have been very tense indeed. After a time the Mattels moved to a separate house across the village, Am Markt 101, thus reducing the population by five, and doubtless lessening the strain to some extent, though the continuing friction between the two older women was the subject of many troubled letters from Wilhelmine to Amalie (who went back to Vienna once her husband returned from his service) and her daughter-in-law, Hermine, for some considerable time following Webern's death.

The knowledge we have of the Weberns' life in Mittersill comes mostly from letters to Hermine, reports elicited by Hans Moldenhauer some years later, particularly a letter to him from Amalie Waller, and from the accounts of the Weberns' neighbour Cesar Bresgen. Bresgen, who was also a musician but with rather different tastes than Webern's, kept a diary of his encounters with Webern in and around Mittersill from their first meeting in the middle of May until Webern's death in September.[15] He records conversations about music and composers, mushrooms, nature, philosophy and the necessities of life. We know from several of these sources that Webern was extremely ill with dysentery for some weeks immediately following his arrival in Mittersill. This was particularly serious in view of the fact that he had been existing under highly stressful conditions and almost certainly suffering from malnutrition as well for a considerable time, and that no medical supplies were available. He did, however, recover during the summer, though he remained much weakened by the experience.

On 30 April Hitler committed suicide; on 7 May German forces surrendered unconditionally. Mittersill was now under American occupation. Four months after the war had ended the Austrian composer Anton Webern, who was universally described by those who knew him as a modest, quiet man of total honesty, a man with the highest ideals and a seeker after peace, became one of its late casualties. The details of his death have been the cause of great speculation, running the gamut from Humphrey Searle's 'stray bullet fired by an Allied soldier'[16] to the theory purportedly held by 'the wife of a noted Viennese composer' that Webern was shot by his own son-in-law Benno Mattel (DAW: 37). The truth, though it will never be known, would seem to lie somewhere between these extremes.

The facts were difficult to come by for several reasons. In the first place, whatever happened occurred at night (no one *saw* anything because it was dark), and then the affair was much complicated by the Weberns having unwittingly been in the midst of an undercover military police operation. There were very few witnesses, and the stories of all of these are unreliable for various reasons, either because of their physical distance from the scene of the shooting (only Webern and the soldier who shot him witnessed the event, and Wilhelmine, who was nearby, was inside the house and in addition was surely in extreme distress when giving her statement) or because they had personal reasons for hiding or distorting certain aspects of the incident (this covers the Mattels, who were being arrested at the time, and the two American soldiers). The only facts about which there appears to have been agreement are the following. The Weberns had been invited to have dinner with the Mattels that evening and had eaten. Webern had been given a cigar earlier by his son-in-law; this was a very great treat in these times of deprivation and Webern had looked forward for some time to the moment after dinner when he would smoke it. The Mattels occupied the ground floor of the house, which consisted of a central hallway running from front to back with the kitchen opening off to the left of this hallway and a room used as sittingroom and bedroom opposite. The family had eaten in the kitchen, and the children had then been put to bed in the other room. Two American soldiers came to the house to see the Mattels after dinner; unbeknownst to the Mattels (and certainly to the Weberns) they had come with the express purpose of catching Benno Mattel in the act of concluding a black-market purchase of American goods (an earlier operation of this sort

16 Christine and Benno Mattel's three children, Karin, Ute and Liese, 1944.

had yielded the cigar that Webern was at that very moment anticipat-
ing with such pleasure); Mattel had been involved in black-market
activities for some time. The soldiers and the Mattels went into the
kitchen to conclude their business, and the Weberns retired to the
room where the children were sleeping. In order not to bother the
children with his smoke Webern stepped outside to smoke part of his
cigar (he intended to save half of it so that he could enjoy it on a later
occasion), and while doing so he was shot three times in the abdomen
and chest. He stumbled back into the sittingroom of the house and
said to his wife, 'I've been shot. It is over' (a pronouncement with a
strong biblical resonance). Upon this skeleton of a tragedy many
forms have been sculpted.

Most accounts have agreed that in stepping outside (about 9.00
according to Wildgans, just after 9.45 according to Wilhelmine, at
10.00 according to Friedrich Herzfeld)[17] Webern was breaking a
curfew. Wildgans says that an 8.00 curfew had recently been imposed
on the civilian population, but that Mattel had not been told of this
because of the plan to trap him that evening. This explanation does

not hold up; Wildgans fails to explain how it was that none of the (ten?) people living in the Halbich household knew about the curfew either. More recent accounts have given a likelier version: that a special curfew had been placed on the house where the Mattels lived for this one occasion only, and that the others living in the house had been told of the curfew but the Mattels naturally had not been, and that it had not occurred to anyone that the Mattels might have visitors that night. A report written by the mayor of Mittersill says that the reason no one was allowed to leave the house was that it was being searched; no curfew is mentioned.

The original story had it that Webern stepped outside the front door and was shot on the porch of the house. (It is an indisputable fact that the three bullet holes are in the front of the house, just to the right of the door.) According to Wildgans, Webern was shot immediately upon stepping through the door. In her police report Wilhelmine said that he had been outside for two or three minutes before he was shot. One story was that when he lit a match this startled a soldier who was outside the house 'staking it out' into shooting him; another said that he only fumbled in his pockets, with the same consequences. Some reports say that Webern was shot without warning, others that a warning was shouted at him which he misunderstood. In 1957 Robert Craft referred to 'Webern's murder – or tragic accident' as an act carried out by a member of 'an occupation unit noted for the precipitancy of its trigger fingers';[18] in 1959 Josef Polnauer wrote that Webern was shot by 'a drunken soldier' (Jone: 92); in 1961 Walter Kolneder described the soldier as 'full of wartime hysteria, obeying orders too rashly'.[19] Hans Rosbaud (who was nowhere near Mittersill at the time) said that Webern was clearly silhouetted in front of the window, thereby suggesting that whoever shot him knew at whom they were shooting; the US army officer who made the original report wrote that 'the blackout curtains were so tightly drawn that hardly a light could be seen from the outside'. Moldenhauer found 'a well-known Swiss composer' whose theory was that Webern's killing was 'intentional', 'a criminal act', and he also quotes Mario Castelnuovo-Tedesco as saying 'Was it an accident? A mistake? Somehow I always doubted it' (DAW: 36–7). Wildgans implies and Herzfeld says outright that it was a question of mistaken identity: that whoever shot Webern thought he was shooting Benno Mattel.

Confusion at every step of the way. In spite of the generally held view that Webern stepped on to the porch and was shot by someone waiting outside covering the house, the original official report does not say this, and if this report is to be believed (and why should it not be?) the presence or absence of curfews and/or warnings has no relevance to the case. The original statement says that after the Mattels were arrested in the kitchen of the house one of the two soldiers left the house to go and get an officer who could place them in official custody, and that as he left the kitchen he bumped into a figure by whom he felt threatened, and whom he shot 'in self defence' (DAW: 85). This has given rise to variations, none stranger than one suggested by David Schroeder in 1996. And it is at this point that our old friend Louis Krasner, that generous purveyor of questionable Webern anecdotes, makes his reappearance. He suggested, in the interview I have referred to before, on what he claimed to be the word of Georg Schoenberg, that Webern's death was suicide. I quote him.

> Now George could not have been a witness to the incident [always a good beginning!] . . . Yet he spoke with absolute certainty as he related a rather different story. It seems that this was known by the inner circle, and they were aware that it contradicted the official version. Webern's sons-in-law were arch-Nazis, you see [This is not true: Fred Halbich was not a Nazi at all, and Gunter Waller could hardly have been called an 'arch-Nazi'], and according to George, one of them was being sought by the Americans as a war criminal [surely a rather grand way of describing a small-time black marketeer]. He was a high official [this was not the case] and still hadn't been found [also untrue, as he lived in the house at Am Markt 101 with his family and everyone knew this]. . . . 'The American soldiers came looking for him,' said George. 'There was a curfew, and in the blackness of night, they approached the house. It was not by chance that Webern came out to smoke. He saw the soldiers and

came outside intentionally to light a match and smoke a cigarette [it was in fact a cigar] – to distract them. Meanwhile, out the rear door, the son-in-law escaped. [It is not true that Mattel escaped; he left the house under arrest and spent the following year in prison.] And in doing this, Webern was shot.

Krasner then goes on to treat us to his skill with invention (of which I think we have probably had numerous samplings already).

I've thought a lot about this, and about how Webern must have felt when he realized that he was fatally wounded. If I were a novelist, I would write a story with a man like Webern as its hero. He would be a man of noble thoughts, absolutely pure in his beliefs and in his desires for the development of culture and humanity. He would become, intellectually, the victim of the Nazis, and suffer the pain of witnessing his own disillusionment and confronting his own fallacies. He would be a very religious man, as was Webern. And I would have his death at the hands of a soldier – through a bullet – be his salvation. At that moment, he would exclaim in his heart, 'Oh, I am saved! I will not have to spend eternity burning in Hell. I was punished on earth. I have salvation and redemption.' Because this is what I believe Webern must have felt. George's views were similar; he called Webern's death 'suicide by third hand'.

Schroeder swallows everything Krasner offers and goes a bit further. In a sort of patchwork of several existing stories he tries to make a case for Webern's actually having provoked the shooting by intentionally bumping into or attacking the soldier in the hallway of the house, thus achieving some sort of atonement for his espousal of the Nazi ideals which had proven to be so wrong and which had in a way been responsible for the death of his own son.[20] A suitably Wagnerian demise, but one which I find unlikely.

Whatever the details of Webern's death actually were, the three gunshots fired at the front door of Am Markt 101 in Mittersill in the late evening of 15 September 1945 put an untimely end to the work of one of this century's most original composers. A romantic, a lyricist, whose creations were often so fleeting that many must have felt through the years as his own father had, that 'they were over before they began'. The creator of moments of the most luminous and beautiful sound. A real innovator holding tightly on to tradition. The discovery of what he had been up to, when the war was over and his music was finally given free hearing, led immediately to one of the most amazing misunderstandings of music history, as the young composers at Darmstadt raised his all-embracing organisation as their banner, ignoring – or perhaps not even knowing – that their hero was a traditionalist who valued and strove above all for comprehensibility in his music. But that is another story; ours ends on 15 September 1945. We have been concerned with the man Webern: a man of passionate loyalties and unresolvable contradictions. A man who was at the same time complex and naïve, whose ardent German nationalism led him to make the most aggressive militaristic statements, yet who was happiest in the peaceful solitude of a mountain plateau surrounded by gentians and wild narcissus, breathing the 'rarefied air of the heights', (in a letter to Berg, dated 4 June 1912), where the quiet was 'something really glorious, really remarkable . . . sublime' (27 December 1908). A man who could demonstrate a fervour of embarrassing intensity for both Schoenberg and Hitler, who throughout his life was given to vitriolic outbursts on the subject of the vulgarity and insensitivity of audiences yet whose entire professional life was spent conducting concerts for 'the people' in socialist Vienna. A man who was described by nearly everyone whose path he crossed as a truly good and honest human being, a devoted husband and father, a loyal friend, a teacher who gave free lessons to gifted students who were too poor to pay when he himself was also destitute. But perhaps most importantly for future generations, the composer of some of the world's loveliest brief moments of music.

17 Last page of Webern's Notebook 6, on which Wilhelmine recorded
Webern's death.

Epilogue

As I opened with a long quotation from Riemerschmid, I should like to close with a long quotation from Dallapiccola, portions of whose Webern diary have been quoted earlier. Dallapiccola, a great admirer of Webern and in my opinion one of his greatest and most musical followers, finally met Webern in 1942, during a stop-over in Vienna. That and subsequent diary entries about Webern and his music seem a fitting close to this little book of Webern's life.

Vienna, March 9, 1942

A stop of twelve or fourteen hours in this dead city is inevitable for anyone who returns from Hungary to Italy. (Two police controls are mandatory.) Nevertheless I am happy, because this evening, in the Schlees' home, I had the good fortune to meet Anton Webern. A mystic, a short man, who talks with some inflection of Austrian dialect: kind, but capable of a burst of anger, cordial to the point of treating me like an equal ('Our common responsibilities', he says).

Without fear, without hesitation by now, we talk about the war. This is among all topics the most urgent, in every country. . . . But we talk also about music. As Webern had not witnessed the immense success of *Das Augenlicht* in London, I tell him about the great impression it made upon me. And Webern immediately asks – 'Were you impressed by the sound also?' (The sound. I understood it correctly.) While discussing problems of orchestral sonorities, the refined researcher (history won't ignore his enormous contribution to the formation of the new language) states: 'A chord of three trumpets or four horns is by now unimaginable to me.'[1]

Incidentally the name of Kurt Weill is mentioned. And Webern suddenly explodes. He points his finger towards me (but I had not been the one who pronounced the name of a composer he dislikes!). And puts to me a very direct question: 'What do you find of our great Middle-European tradition in such a composer? . . . that tradition which includes the names (and here he starts to enumerate them on his fingers) of Schubert, Brahms, Wolf, Mahler, Schönberg, Berg and myself?'

I was embarrassed. I do not say that an answer would not be possible; but what confounds me most is that Webern used the term 'tradition', a term which knowing the *Variations Op.* 21, the Cantata *Das Augenlicht*, and, even through a single audition, the *Concerto Op.* 24, I supposed had been eliminated from Webern's vocabulary. Not only that. But that he should consider himself as an heir to the tradition; that he should believe in the continuity of language.[2] . . . And finally that what separated him from Kurt Weill should not be a question of aesthetics and of taste, but rather the fact that Kurt Weill had refused the Middle-European tradition.

Webern impressed me very much also as a human being. And I think again of what Theodor Wiesengrund Adorno wrote about him years ago: 'The assault which Schoenberg's constructivity moved against the walled doors of musical objectivism is (in the songs Op. 14 and 15) just a vibration which comes to us from extreme distances. It is a solitary soul who trembles before the walled doors, and clings to faith: nothing else is left.'

Fiesole, Dec. 3, 1943

Today Anton Webern is sixty years old. *A solitary soul who clings to faith.* . . . In Florence, as by now in all Italian cities, persecution takes a perturbing rhythm. I feel myself, more than ever, *a solitary soul* . . .

I decide to dedicate to the Master the six *Carmine Alcaei*, which I am going to present him, when the war is over, with the trepidation well known to one who submits his own work to the judgement of somebody so far his superior.

Florence, Oct. 22, 1945
From Vienna, dated Oct.8, a friend writes me: 'unfortunately I also have to give you some extremely sad news: Webern died in a tragic accident, just now when his work would finally have received a definite recognition among us . . .'

Florence, Oct. 22, 1945
The six *Carmine Alcaei* will be dedicated, in humility and devotion, to his memory.[3]

Prologue

1 This document is in the Paul Sacher Stiftung in Basel.
2 Anschluß: the annexation of Austria by Hitler in 1938.

1 1883–1902 Childhood and school years

1 This is the spelling that appears on all family documents: the birth
certificate of both Webern and his mother, and the marriage
certificates of Webern's parents and his maternal grandparents.
(These documents are at the Paul Sacher Stiftung (hereafter PSS)
in Basel.) Both Wildgans and Krellmann use the spelling Gehr.
2 These notebooks will be referred to hereafter as Nb1, Nb2 etc.
Notebooks 1–8 are owned by the PSS; an additional one, which I
shall identify as Nb9, is in the Wiener Stadt- und Landesbibliothek.
3 Joseph Joachim Raff, b. near Zurich, 1822; d. Frankfurt am Main,
1882. German composer and teacher, friend of von Bülow and Liszt
and on the editorial staff of the Neue Zeitschrift für Musik, 1854–61. 'Im
Walde', written in 1869, was the third of eleven symphonies.
4 It is curious that he describes the movements in this order without
comment. In the absence of the finale the order of the two inner
movements must have been reversed so that the piece would end
with a fast movement.
5 Susanne Rode-Breymann explores more fully Webern's relationship
with these poets in ' ". . . gathering the divine from the earthly . . . ":
Ferdinand Avernarius and his Significance for Anton Webern's Early

Settings of Lyric Poetry', in *Webern Studies*, ed. K. Bailey (Cambridge: Cambridge University Press, 1996).

6 Hans Moldenhauer published all but the second of these songs in 1965, rather against the wishes of Maria Halbich, who believes her father's judgement should have been respected.

7 I can think of no successful translation of this word in this situation for British readers. In America 'Matura' would be translated as 'graduation'; in Britain this event is called 'school-leaving', but there is no way to incorporate the latter term into Webern's note.

2 1902–8 *Shaping forces*

1 These letters survive and have been quoted widely (large excerpts appear in both Wildgans and Moldenhauer); for this reason they will not be quoted here.

2 'Diez' was Max Dietz, who lectured on the history of German and Italian opera in Webern's first term. Webern did not enrol for any further lectures by Dietz during subsequent years; Theophil Antonicek of the University of Vienna suggests that Webern may have been influenced in this by Adler's low opinion of Dietz's competence. Adler was the head of the university's Institute of Musicology and Webern's advisor. Nevertheless Wallaschek, who was also no friend of Adler, appears to have been one of Webern's favourites: Webern signed on for three of his courses. (For information concerning Webern's university career I am indebted to Professor Antonicek, who kindly supplied me with a copy of his unpublished paper, 'Anton Webern und die Musikwissenschaft'.)

3 Webern was soon to give up his cello study altogether. He continued to play the piano all his life, though Wildgans describes him as 'a fairly poor piano player' who could read at sight but never practised technique (Wildgans, *Anton Webern*, p. 34). Maria Halbich says that to his family he always seemed a very good pianist.

4 This piece did not, however, appear in the DTÖ, and according to Antonicek no copy of the piece in Webern's hand has ever been found in the DTÖ archives, though there is in the archives a transcription of five songs by Senfl in his hand; these also were not published in the DTÖ.

5 According to Antonicek Adler's class list for this year contains eighteen names, and there were not four Poles: Webern was either confused about the nationality of a man named Koczirz, whom he hardly knew, or one of his Poles was also one of his Jews. In either case Webern does not enumerate the entire class. Antonicek assumes that when Webern writes of Germans, he means 'German-speaking' students, i.e. Germans and Austrians.

6 Austrian conductor, b. Graz, 1846; d. near Dresden, 1914. Schuch studied law in Graz, then music in Vienna. In 1872 he moved to Dresden, where he was responsible for making the Dresden opera and orchestra musical organisations of the first rank.

7 I am grateful to Morten Solvik for finding me the programmes for this season. The eighth concert consisted of a Mozart symphony, Weber's overture to *Oberon* and the Fourth Symphony of Beethoven. Other works performed in this series but not mentioned by Webern were two Beethoven overtures – *Egmont* and the *Ruins of Athens* – and Dukas' *Sorcerer's Apprentice*.

8 In later life Webern never conducted either the Brahms Third Symphony or Schumann's Fourth.

9 'Italian national music', in *Style and Idea*, ed. Leonard Stein, trans. Leo Black (London: Faber & Faber, 1975), p. 175.

10 Pfingsten is the Whitsun school vacation.

11 I can not read this word.

12 Antonicek suggests that the difficulty over Webern's dissertation may have had less to do with Webern than with Adler, for whom this situation was not uncommon. His untempered enthusiasm for his own students in the face of their often indifferent performance in other areas, as well as a certain degree of antisemitism on the part of his colleagues, resulted in this sort of obstruction on several occasions.

13 For a discussion of this question see Derrick Puffett, 'Gone with the summer wind; or, what Webern lost', in K. Bailey, ed., *Webern Studies*, pp. 32–73.

14 See the group of essays that form Part III ('Folk-music and nationalism') of Schoenberg's *Style and Idea* (pp. 161–76).

15 The *Harmonielehre*, written in 1911, and the later *Structural Functions*

of Harmony and *Fundamentals of Musical Composition*, both written in
California in the 1940s.

3 1908–14 Instability makes itself known

1 In this concert, henceforth to be known universally as the
  Skandalkonzert, Webern's pieces were greeted with a storm of laughter
  and followed by a confrontation between opposing factions of the
  audience, Schoenberg's Chamber Symphony elicited jeers and
  catcalls, and finally during the performance of Berg's *Altenberg Lieder*
  the occasion was reduced to one of total mayhem, with audience and
  composers alike shouting insults, and disagreements between
  members of the audience erupting into physical violence. The stage
  and musicians were stormed by the angry audience, the police were
  called and the *Kindertotenlieder* were never performed. The theatre
  director pleaded for silence to show respect for Mahler in allowing
  his work to be heard; one critic later opined that Mahler's memory
  had been honoured by his work *not* having been performed on such
  a programme.
2 Salka Viertel, *The Kindness of Strangers* (New York: Holt, Rinehart and
  Winton, 1969), p. 57.

4 1914–21 Vacillations continue

1 Maria Halbich has said that her father hated playing cards, but that
  he was forced by the domineering Schoenberg to do it every day.
2 Willi Reich, *Schoenberg: A Critical Biography*, trans. Leo Black (London:
  Longman, 1971), p. 122.
3 Walter Szmolyan, 'Die Konzerte des Wiener Schönberg-Vereins',
  Österreichische Musikzeitschrift 36 (February 1981), pp. 84–102; his
  information is reproduced in translation in Joan Allen Smith,
  Schoenberg and His Circle (London: Collier Macmillan, 1986),
  pp. 255–68.
4 In true Webern fashion, the list of gifts for Maria (who was five years
  old in 1918) goes through two revisions before it appears in its
  definitive form. At first there is to be a pocket knife and a book of
  maps from her father, a pencil and pencil sharpener and a handbag

from her mother, an bracelet, a school bag (this has been crossed
out) and a doll's coat. Eventually the list evolved so that there were
seven gifts for each of the girls and four for Peter (who would have
been three years old in 1918 and was scheduled to receive a sweater,
a game, a picture book and a drum).

5   1922–8   Changes of direction

1 Although he had been rehearsal and second conductor in provincial
theatres off and on for the decade before this he had never had any
experience at conducting concerts. His repertoire had been confined
(as he continually made plain to all his friends and correspondents)
to second-rate operettas and the like; he had had no opportunity to
conduct the symphonic repertoire.

2 The events in the preceding paragraph occurred in the years 1923–8;
the records are found in pp. 4–59 of the notebook.

3 The events in this paragraph are recorded in pp. 28–98 of the
notebook.

4 Nb6, pp. 46–8.

5 Nb6, pp. 21–2.

6 The Workers' Symphony Concerts (Arbeiter-Symphonie-Konzerte)
had been instituted in 1905 by David Josef Bach, a contemporary of
Schoenberg and an active socialist dedicated to making the arts
accessible to the working classes. Bach became the editor-in-chief
of the literature and art section of the *Arbeiterzeitung* in 1917 and was
active in the Arts Council once the Social Democratic Party came
to power in 1919.

7 Rosegger (1843–1918) came from one of the alpine regions that
Webern held most dear and shared Webern's passion for the
purifying isolation of the mountains. His collected works run to forty
volumes. In 1912 Webern wrote to Berg: 'I tell you, he [Rosegger] is
the greatest living German poet'.

8 Anne C. Shreffler identifies the sources of these texts in '"Mein Weg
geht jetzt vorüber": the vocal origins of Webern's twelve-tone
composition', *Journal of the American Musicological Society* 47/2 (1994),
p. 321. The fact that Webern does not identify them is interesting: he
probably thought they were all folksongs. Certainly that from *Des
Knaben Wunderhorn* is, but it was Rosegger's habit to lace his stories

and novels with what appeared to be folksong texts though they
were in fact his own inventions. See Peter Andraschke, 'Webern
und Rosegger', in *Opus Anton Webern*, ed. Dieter Rexroth (Berlin:
Quadriga, 1983), pp. 108–10.

9 Webern seems to be in error about the date of this concert: all other
sources agree that it took place on 5 June.

10 In 1913 Prince Max Egon zu Fürstenberg founded the Gesellschaft
für Musik Freunde in Donaueschingen, out of which grew the
Donaueschingen Festival, which took place for the first time in 1921.
Though the later Donaueschingen festival was organised by the
Gesellschaft der Musikfreunde Donaueschingen, Fürstenberg
remained its chief patron, and concerts took place in the Fürstenberg
castle. This was the earliest festival to be devoted exclusively to
contemporary music.

11 Shreffler, '"Mein Weg geht jetzt vorüber"' pp. 282–3.

12 H. H. Stuckenschmidt, *Arnold Schoenberg: His Life, World and Work*,
trans. Humphrey Searle (London: John Calder, 1977), p. 443.

13 The twelve-note technique provides a means of structuring and
unifying a composition in the absence of tonality. An entire
composition is based on a single arrangement of the twelve notes
of the chromatic scale (the row) and its various permutations. Once
the order of the notes has been set, the row can be inverted or played
backwards, or both these operations can be applied simultaneously.
Each of these four versions of the row (the original form, its
inversion, its retrograde and its retrograde inversion) can be
transposed to begin on any of the twelve notes of the scale; this yields
forty-eight distinct versions of the row. Rows are then arranged as
melodies and chords and are used to produce all the conventional
musical textures: they can be expressed horizontally or vertically,
and several permutations may proceed at the same time, but in strict
twelve-note music each row must produce its twelve notes in the
prescribed order. Thus, while in theory there is no predominance
of any note comparable to that of the tonic note in tonal music, there
is usually a predominance of certain intervals – those between
adjoining notes in the row, because while the sequence of pitches
changes when the row undergoes transposition or permutation,
the sequence of intervals remains stable. A further refinement that

particularly fascinated Schoenberg was combinatoriality, the production of a row in such a way that the hexachordal content of one or more of its permutations complemented that of the original row (i.e. the first six notes of the original row – its first hexachord – were the last six notes of the combinatorial permutation(s)); two permutations that exhibit this complementary relationship can be played at the same time with a minimum of pitch duplication.

14 The Workers' Symphony Concerts, particularly those in November, were usually in celebration of something or someone, and frequently had a socialist or republican slant. The November concerts of 1926 commemorated the death in 1918 of Victor Adler, an important figure in the history of Austrian socialism.

15 One has to rely on Moldenhauer's word for these dates, as this is the only twelve-note work of Webern's for which the sketches are not available, being still privately owned. As we have seen, Webern had conducting engagements on 8 January, 19 and 31 March and 1 May of 1927.

16 As Schoenberg seemed usually to turn to the piano at critical stages of his composition (one thinks for example of the first piece to shun rather aggressively both tonality and motives, the third of his Three Piano Pieces, Op. 11; his only aphorisms, the Six Little Pieces of Op. 19; the Five Piano Pieces, Op. 23, in which he was obviously working his way up to the twelve-note technique through experiments with various other types of serialism; the first strict demonstrations of the possibilities of combinatoriality – combinatorial tetrachords in the Op. 25 Suite for Piano and hexachordal combinatoriality in the two Piano Pieces of Op. 33). Webern turned to the song in times of crisis.

17 I am not going to translate the title of this organisation into English, as I can find no one who knows exactly what it means. It would suggest that the chorus was made up of non-union typographers, or perhaps of members of a typographers' union that was independent from other printing unions, but even in Vienna it is difficult to find exact information about this.

18 This term, borrowed from painting, where many individual dots of pure colours are blended by the eye to form a shaded form, is used to describe in music the use of a succession of individual notes played on different instruments and in different registers to produce a

single melodic line. The intended whole is much more difficult to perceive in the musical version of this technique than in the visual.

19 Maria Halbich, who was a young teenager at the time, also has no clear memory of the meeting. She says only that she thinks it took place in the mid 1920s and is rather certain that Berg introduced them.

6 1929–33 The path to new music

1 Nb6, pp. 59, 74, 78–80, 89–90.

2 Nb6, pp. 98, 99, 101.

3 It is curious that Webern ceased to use this diary when he did. It is clear that it must have been taken to Mittersill when the family fled there, because Wilhelmine recorded Webern's death, on 15 September 1945, on the last page (see Plate 17 on p. 192). There are many blank pages in the book.

4 The philosopher and sociologist Theodor Wiesengrund Adorno (1903–69), who had studied composition with Berg.

5 Although Webern gives 5 March as the date of this concert (on pp. 77 and 83), other sources give the date as 4 March.

6 This is a famous palindrome with a long history. The letters can also be arranged as two statements of A[lpha] PATER NOSTER O[mega], one vertical and the other horizontal, crossing with the letter N as the crux (as it is also in the SATOR AREPO arrangement).

7 1933–8 Before the Anschluß

1 The programme on this occasion was Webern's Op. 2 chorus, *Entflieht auf leichten Kähnen*; Five Movements for String Quartet, Op. 5; the Op. 7 pieces for violin and piano; Three Little Pieces for Cello and Piano, Op. 11; and songs from Opp. 3, 4 and 12.

2 Mathilde Schoenberg had died in 1923 and in the following year Schoenberg had married Gertrud Kolisch, sister of the violinist and Schoenberg student Rudolf Kolisch. They were to have three children; the first, a daughter, Nuria, was born in 1932.

3 This was not the first time Webern had submitted a work to someone in the US, but it was now particularly critical for him to get a work accepted outside German Europe, as his music could no longer be published in Vienna.

4 Louis Krasner, interviewed by Don C. Seibert, 'Some memories of
Anton Webern, the Berg Concerto, and Vienna in the 1930s', *Fanfare*
11/2 (1987), pp. 335–47 (p. 347).

5 The circumstances of the trip to Barcelona and the concert there are
related by Krasner in Seibert, 'Some memories of Anton Webern',
pp. 335–40.

6 'Personal recollections of Webern in Vienna 1929–1934', *Congress
Webern Beiträge 1972/73*, Österreichischen Gesellschaft für Musik
(Kassel: Bärenreiter, 1973), p. 32.

7 The Schubert is a recording of the Frankfurt Radio Orchestra on 29
December 1932. I have only heard it on tape. The historic
performance of the Concerto is on a Continuum CD (SBT 1004).

8 1938–45 *After the Anschluß*

1 In Seibert, 'Some memories of Anton Webern', p. 343.

2 Indeed, one wonders if this legendary letter is not the letter of
1 January 1934 quoted above on p. 154.

3 *Anton Webern*, p. 110.

4 This must refer to the German invasion of Denmark and Norway
in April 1940. Denmark was occupied on 9 April without formal
resistance; Norway resisted until 30 April, falling just days before
Webern's letter to Hueber.

5 Japan's method of entering the war should be borne in mind.

6 By this time Hong Kong and Singapore had fallen to the Japanese, as
had the Philippines and most of the rest of the islands of the Pacific
west of Hawaii.

7 In the *Sunday Telegraph*, April 1961, and reproduced as Translator's
Preface to Wildgans, *Anton Webern*, p. 11.

8 Fred Prieberg, 'Die krummen Rücken', in *Musik und Macht* (Frankfurt
am Main: Fischer Taschenbuchverlag, 1991), pp. 225–79. (I do not
translate Reichsmusikkammer in subsequent references, as any
translation is either unwieldy or it loses some meaning.)

9 Stuckenschmidt, *Arnold Schoenberg*, p. 134.

10 *Style and Idea*, p. 505.

11 According to Maria Halbich. Moldenhauer describes him as blond-
haired and blue-eyed.

12 Bailey, *The Twelve-note Music of Anton Webern* (Cambridge: Cambridge University Press, 1991), p. 331.

13 Personal communication from David Lewin. Before their publication Webern sent Steuermann a specially copied manuscript of the Variations bearing the following dedication: 'With heartfelt greetings and best wishes from your A. W., Christmas 1936'. (This copy is now in the Pierpont Morgan Library in New York.) It has been reported that when asked Steuermann claimed it was for 'personal reasons' that he did not perform the Op. 27 Variations. His reasons have been interpreted variously: everyone agrees that political differences were important, but whereas Moldenhauer sees these as the sole impediment, Steuermann's student Russell Sherman has suggested that Steuermann also did not find Webern's later style of composition particularly to his taste and that he found the Piano Variations 'a little dry' (Regina Busch, 'Aus dem Briefwechsel Webern–Steuermann', in *Anton Webern I*, ed. Heinz-Klaus Metzger and Rainer Riehn, Musik-Konzepte Sonderband (Munich: Edition Text+Kritik, 1983), p. 48n).

14 This was Lawrence, the first son of Schoenberg's second family.

15 Cesar Bresgen, *Mittersill 1934 – Ein Weg zu Anton von Webern* (Vienna: Österreichischer Bundesverlag, 1983).

16 Humphrey Searle, 'Webern's last works', *The Monthly Musical Record* xx (December 1946), p. 231.

17 'Anton Weberns Tod', *Neue Zeitschrift für Musik* 119 (1958), p. 147.

18 In his notes to his recording of Webern's complete works for Columbia.

19 In the original German version of his *Anton Webern*.

20 David Schroeder, 'Not proven', *The Musical Times* xx (June 1996), pp. 21–3.

Epilogue

1 In this remark Webern makes a very subtle distinction concerning colour. In his Second Cantata, which he was in the midst of composing at this time, there are many four-note chords played by horn, trumpet, trombone and tuba, as well as chords of many more notes, played by combined brass and woodwind. What Webern was

referring to as 'unimaginable' was not the use of a chord of wind instruments, but of a group of like instruments playing together: three trumpets or four horns.

2 [Dallapiccola's note, added at a later time:] What in 1942 seemed to me incomprehensible, is clear today to all who are familiar with the work of Anton Webern. Without any effort we see today how much he owes to the tradition, to the 'Ländler'; and it won't be too difficult, listening by transparency as it were, to the first page of the Symphony Op. 21, to realise that, in spite of all differences, it might be regarded as the last echo of the beginning of the Fourth Symphony by Brahms.

3 All the Dallapiccola diary entries cited here were first published in Il Mondo (Florence), 3 November 1945.

No theoretical or analytical studies of Webern's music appear in this bibliography: a complete list of these to 1995 can be found in Zoltan Roman, 'Selected bibliography', in Moldenhauer, *Anton von Webern*, pp. 757–73, and Neil Boynton, 'A Webern bibliography', in *Cambridge Webern Studies*, ed. K. Bailey (Cambridge: Cambridge University Press, 1996), pp. 324–62. The following list of books and articles contains general biographies as well as a few more detailed studies of various aspects of Webern's life that have been touched upon in the preceding pages.

In English:

Berg, Alban. *Letters to his Wife*. Edited, translated and annotated by Bernard Grun. London: Faber and Faber, 1971

Brand, Juliane, Christopher Hailey and Donald Harris, eds. *The Berg–Schoenberg Correspondence*. London: Macmillan, 1987

Kolneder, Walter. *Anton Webern: An Introduction to his Works*. Translated by Humphrey Searle. London: Faber and Faber, 1968

Moldenhauer, Hans and Rosaleen. *Anton von Webern: A Chronicle of his Life and Work*. London: Victor Gollancz, 1978

Moldenhauer, Hans. *The Death of Anton Webern: A Drama in Documents*. New York: Philosophical Library, 1961

Smith, Joan Allen. *Schoenberg and his Circle: A Viennese Portrait*. New York: Collier Macmillan, 1986

Stuckenschmidt, H. H. *Arnold Schoenberg: His Life, World and Work*. Translated by Humphrey Searle. London: John Calder, 1977

Webern, Anton. *Letters to Hildegard Jone and Josef Humplik*. Edited by Josef Polnauer. Bryn Mawr: Theodore Presser, 1967

Webern, Anton. *The Path to the New Music*. Edited by Willi Reich and translated by Leo Black. London: Universal Edition, 1975

Wildgans, Friedrich. *Anton Webern*. Translated by Edith Temple Roberts and Humphrey Searle. London: Calder and Boyars, 1966

In German:

Busch, Regina. 'Verzeichnis der von Webern dirigierten und einstudierten Werke', *Anton Webern II*, ed. Heinz-Klaus Metzger and Rainer Riehn, Musik-Konzepte Sonderband (Munich: Edition Text+Kritik, 1984). Pp. 398ff

Hilmar, Ernst, ed. *Anton Webern 1883–1983*. Vienna: Universal Edition, 1983

Krellmann, Hanspeter. *Anton Webern in Selbstzeugnissen und Bilddokumenten*. Reinbek bei Hamburg: Rowohlt Taschenbuch Verlag, 1975

Webern, Anton. *Weg und Gestalt mit Photos und Dokumenten*. Edited by Willi Reich. Zurich: Verlag der Arche, 1961

Zemlinsky, Alexander. *Zemlinskys Briefwechsel mit Schönberg, Webern, Berg und Schreker*. Edited by Horst Weber. Darmstadt: Wissenschaftliche Buchgesellschaft, 1995

INDEX